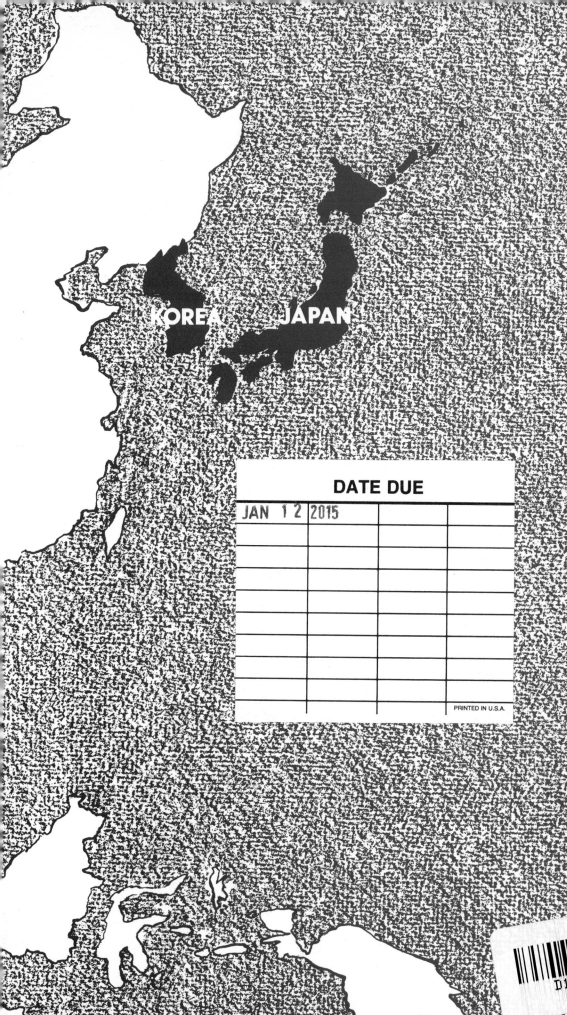

KOREA   JAPAN

DATE DUE

JAN 1 2 2015			

PRINTED IN U.S.A.

FOODS of the ORIENT

JAPAN & KOREA

Introduced by Derek Davies

ENIGMA

Picture Credits

Desjardins/Top	9(T)
Alan Duns	16, 90
Burt Glinn/Magnum	10
J. Hillelson/Roland Michaud	6(B)
Paul Kemp	45, 95
Peter Larsen	6(T)
E. Miyazawa/Black Star	9(B)
Roger Phillips	13, 23, 28, 32, 35, 53, 60, 64, 66, 71, 76/7, 81, 85, 98
David Smith	48, 57

Edited by Isabel Moore
and Jonnie Godfrey
Published by Marshall Cavendish Books Limited
58 Old Compton Street
London W1V 5PA

Printed in Great Britain

ISBN 0 85685 484 0

CONTENTS

INTRODUCTION Derek Davies

TO JAPAN & KOREA

Neither Japanese nor Korean cuisine is much known outside its own shores, although with increasing travel, especially to Japan, this will probably change. Those lucky enough to have tasted food from Japan and Korea know them to be delicious and unique, but the majority, who have not, assume them to be more or less the same and both rather poor relations of the magnificent cuisine of China. Nothing could be farther from the truth for while there are similarities (many ingredients are common to all three, they all use chopsticks and rice is the basic staple), there are also enormous differences (methods of preparation and cooking, the flavours preferred). They are related to one another, in fact, only as the French, British and Spanish cuisines are inter-related.

In general, Japanese food is delicate and refined, with an emphasis on freshness and clean, sharp, natural tastes: hot, spicy flavourings, popular in India and Malaysia are not used. Many ingredients, fish in particular, are eaten uncooked, and dipping sauces are used extensively to enhance the flavours. Not only are subtleties of taste all important, but the appearance of the dish should satisfy the eye just as much as the flavours satisfy the palate. Korean food, with a strong, rather spicy character of its own, also 'borrows' what is considered to be the best of neighbouring cuisines – so you will find Chinese noodles happily married to a dish containing Japanese soy sauce, and even a dish called 'curry', which turns out to be hot and spicy and with a chilli base.

The two most important ingredients in both cuisines are rice and soya beans. Plain rice is served with all meals. In Japan it has an almost religious significance and shrines to the rice god, *Inari*, can be seen throughout the country. Historically, it was used as a unit of taxation and as a measure of man's wealth; even today, so important is its preparation, that a women's skill at cooking is judged according to how well she makes it. Rice is also used to make wine: in Korea, known as *mah koli*, and in Japan, *sake* and *mirin*, not only drunk but also used extensively in cooking.

The versatile soya bean makes its appearance in several forms: it is the basic ingredient of soy sauce, which is the foundation of all Korean and Japanese cooking (it is used not only as a dipping sauce and as a seasoning, but as part of the base mixture in which many ingredients are cooked); it is con-verted into the white, jelly-like bean curd cake called *tofu* in Japan, which turns up in all sorts of dishes and in many different forms; and it is made into *miso*, a fermented paste used to marinate and dress fish and vegetables, and as a base for a whole range of soups.

Meat has always been part of the Korean diet, if something of a luxury, and several national dishes boast beef in various guises, but the Japanese ate it only rarely until about a hundred years ago. Partly, this was the result of Buddhist proscriptions against eating anything that had 'received the breath of life' and partly because the mountainous islands of Japan lacked suitable grazing land for the breeding of cattle. At the end of the nineteenth century, however, Japan was opened to the West after more than 200 years of isolation and the diet, among many other things, changed dramatically. As part of the general adoption of Western ways, people were positively encouraged to eat meat. Most Japanese meat dishes, in fact, date from this time, including the popular *sukiyaki*. Reservations about meat do still remain in respect to lamb, which is rarely eaten.

For both the Japanese and Koreans, the most important source of protein is the sea. Favourable currents in the surrounding waters, long coastlines and numerous islands endow both with a wealth of marine life. The Japanese eat more fish per head of the population than any other people in the world: nearly half a kilo or a pound each per week. They also eat a wide variety including, on occasions, strange species such as sea-urchins and deadly blow-fish (*fugu*). (Blow-fish are prepared in restaurants specially licensed to remove the poison – but even so a number of Japanese people die from *fugu* poisoning each year.) The Japanese are particuarly ingenious at cooking and preparing fish and shell-fish: an old text describes a hundred ways of preparing one fish alone, the *tai*, or sea bream, much appreciated by the Japanese and always eaten on festive occasions.

Fish is not the only seafood eaten in Japan, however, seaweeds – or more accurately sea vegetables such as *nori* (laver) and *kombu* (kelp) – are used extensively. They are eaten primarily for their flavour which is rich and subtle, but they also contain a high proportion of iodine and vitamins, which makes them beneficial to health as well. *Nori* is specially prepared in thin, dried sheets which

can be used as a sort of delicate wrapping material
for many foods, or as a garnish for soups and rice
dishes. Its flavour is enhanced when heated until
dry and brittle, and then it is quite delicious simply
dipped in a soy sauce and eaten with rice. *Kombu* is
also dried into sheets, but thicker and harder ones
than *nori* and they are used mainly in soups and
stocks – Japanese *dashi* (stock) is made from *kombu*
and the flakes of dried bonito fish (*katsuobushi*). In
contrast, the Koreans usually make soups and
stocks with a meat base. Seaweed is not part of their
diet, though it is cultivated for export to Japan.

Apart from their great range of seafoods, Japan
and Korea also possess a wealth of fruit and
vegetables. Korea is a mainly agricultural country
where most of the world's common vegetables are
grown, as well as some unusual roots, leaves and
edible mosses. Koreans say that without vegetables,
no meal is complete. As for Japan, the sheer length
of the country – over a thousand miles from north
to south – as well as a varied topography and
pronounced seasons, create climatic differences
conducive to great variety.

In keeping with their love of nature, the Japanese
pay great attention to seasonal changes. Not only
do fruit and vegetables have their seasons, but even
cakes and tea.

Winter is the time for tangerines, hot noodles
and warming one-pot dishes cooked on the table;
in February the world's largest and most succulent
strawberries make their appearance; with the
spring and the first sound of the nightingale come
cakes shaped like nightingales; and as the cherry
blossom begins to flower, cakes flavoured with
cherry blossoms also appear. Spring is also the time
for tender bamboo shoots and the mellow flavour
of new tea, *shincha*.

May sees the opening of the season for the *ayu*, a
small, delicious and delicately flavoured river trout.
In one part of Japan, Gifu, there is an ingenious
method of catching *ayu*: cormorants tethered to
fishing boats snatch the fish from the water, and are
then pulled back on to the boats by the fishermen
where they disgorge their catch. Summer is also the
time for chilled noodles, chilled *tofu* and hot eels.

Autumn (fall) is the season for pickle making. In
Korea, the markets are laden with large, white
radishes, Chinese cabbages, hot red peppers and
dozens of other vegetables that go into the many
varieties of *kim chee*. All domestic activity centres
on the business of chopping and sorting vegetables
and filling the pickle pots for winter. 'When the

kim chee is prepared for the winter,' they say,
'half the harvest is done.' The Japanese also make
and eat many pickles, although generally they are
gentler than the Korean variety. In Japan, autumn
is also the season for what are said to be the world's
most delicious mushrooms, the *matsutake*. During
the season, city dwellers equipped with cooking
gear converge on the forests where the mushrooms
grow to picnic on them.

One of the great pleasures of travelling in both
countries is the variety of their regional specialities.
Each town or area has its own products, from
handicrafts such as lacquerware or pottery, to
various foods, such as cakes, pickles and fish. A
Japanese island might be noted for abalone (*awabe*),
which is collected from the seabed by specially-
trained diving girls; or a mountain village might be
famous for its young fern shoots (*warabi*). But
apart from such special products, the taste of food
varies from region to region. In Japan, the food of
Kyoto tends to be lighter and more subtle than
that of Tokyo, reflecting perhaps the tastes of the
old Kyoto court. With its many Buddhist temples,
Kyoto is also famous for its vegetarian dishes, while
Tokyo, with its huge fish market, is known for the
flavour of its seafood. The long trading history of
Nagasaki in the southern island has left strong
Chinese influences on the food of that region.

It was in the imperial courts of Kyoto and Nara
that the tea ceremony was developed from its
Chinese origins into a stylized ritual. Today, the
tea ceremony is still widely practised, and know-
ledge of it is considered to be an important qualifi-
cation for prospective Japanese brides. Essentially,
the tea ceremony is the art of preparing tea as
gracefully as possible, but the manner in which it is
done is highly formalized. Practitioners must
strictly observe the correct procedures, such as
how to pour the water and hold the tea bowl. Tea
ceremony food, *kaiseki*, is the most refined of the
Japanese cuisine, with great emphasis being placed
upon simplicity and harmony. The tastes, textures
and colours of the food should balance one another,
and the containers in which it is served should
enhance its appearance. *Kaiseki* food reflects the
seasons and, if possible, is locally produced; it
should not be expensive or extravagant, but should
be imaginative and in good taste. The tea used for
the tea ceremony is a special type of powdered
green tea, *matcha*. After adding hot water to the
powder, it is whipped with a bamboo whisk which
looks rather like a shaving brush. The taste is
bitter, but refreshing.

The Koreans have no equivalent of the Japanese
tea ceremony, though they are enthusiastic tea
drinkers. They do, however, have a special tea
made from the roots of the *ginsing* plant. *Ginsing* tea
is rich to taste and is reputed to have many
medicinal properties. They also make a rice tea
from the grains remaining in the saucepan after the

rice has been cooked.

To describe the ingredients of a nation's cooking, particularly when many of them are strange to the western palate, can be misleading – the thought of eating uncooked fish, for example, is repugnant to many, but when it is eaten absolutely fresh, in the Japanese manner, you can almost forget that it is fish at all; the tastes and textures might best be compared to chilled, very tender, rare beef. And many who have tried uncooked fish dishes, such as *sushi* and *sashimi*, consider them to be among the greatest delicacies in Japan's vast cuisine.

Other dishes are less difficult: *tempura*, for example, deep-fried vegetables and fish in the lightest of batters, is popular throughout the world. Properly prepared, it is succulent and crisp with only the slightest hint of oil. Strangely enough although it is one of the country's best-known dishes, it is not strictly speaking Japanese at all – but an adaptation of a Portuguese dish. (It arrived with Western traders and missionaries over four hundred years ago and the name itself comes from the Latin word for time – a reference to those certain days of the year on which the Portuguese, as good Catholics, could not eat meat.) Another dish easy to appreciate is *sukiyaki*, thinly sliced beef cooked in one-pot style on the table.

Sukiyaki and *tempura* are served both at home and in restaurants, or are delivered from the restaurants to the home – a common practice in Japan. This is because, on the whole, restaurants are better equipped to prepare the food properly – the cutting of the fish for *sushi*, for example, requires great skill, and *sushi* cooks are required to spend many years in apprenticeship. Some restaurants serve only one type of food, such as *tempura*, *noodles* or *sushi*, and there are even some which serve only *tofu* dishes. The Japanese never drink without eating and many dishes can therefore be regarded primarily as snacks with alcohol – even the smallest bars serve their own specialities. The Koreans also make many snack dishes to be served with drinks, some of them quite unusual – bulls' testicles, which are thought to be a powerful aphrodisiac, are very popular!

For both Japanese and Korean meals, the dishes are not served consecutively in courses as they are in the West, but are placed together on the table. The Koreans arrange the dishes on low tables in the kitchen and then carry them to the eating area. Almost invariably every Japanese and Korean meal includes rice and soup, perhaps a main dish of meat or fish, dipping sauces and various side dishes. Usually there will be separate dishes and bowls for each person. There are no rules about the order in which the food is eaten, though it is customary to sip a little of the soup first. Some hot dishes, such as *tempura* or *shin-sol-lo* should be eaten as soon as they are served. Very often, if people are drinking *sake* with the meal, they will not eat rice until they

Dinner – in the traditional Japanese way, cross-legged on the floor below a low table.

have finished drinking. The meal is usually completed by rice, pickles and tea. Desserts are not a part of either Japanese or Korean cooking, though sometimes fresh fruit will be served at the end of a meal.

The style of a one-pot meal is somewhat different, however, for all the ingredients are prepared in the kitchen in advance and the cooking done on a portable burner on the centre of the dining table. Each person selects what he or she wants from the plates of uncooked ingredients and places them in the communal pot. After brief cooking, the food is transferred to a dipping sauce before eating. The cooking time is so short that the flavour, texture and essential nutrients of the ingredients are not destroyed. A one-pot meal is ideal for dinner parties since it does not take long to prepare or cook, and is informal to eat. A selection of ingredients to make up a first batch to be put in the pot, is put on the table and, when these are eaten, there is traditionally a pause while conversation and drinking take over from food. Later, more rounds can be cooked, with further rests between them. The portable burner may be of any type, so long as it is powerful enough to bring the cooking liquid to boiling point. The Japanese have a variety of dishes known as *nabes* (pots), after which many one-pot dishes are named, but any type of flameproof pot, or fondue pot is equally suitable. The Koreans have a special charcoal stove, called *shin-sol-lo*, used to cook their national dish. It is shaped rather like a hat: the charcoal is placed in the middle and the cooking liquid in the surrounding brim.

In spite of the emphasis that is placed on appearance, it is a mistake to assume that Japanese and Korean food is expensive to prepare at home. Elaborate garnishes and beautiful pottery are not necessary, and more often than not they can be omitted from home cooking: you can improvise very well with soup or cereal bowls, or even decorative ashtrays. Many of the ingredients are relatively cheap, though obviously some special ones are necessary for certain dishes. Very often substitutes are quite acceptable, while other dishes can be made from ingredients commonly available at grocery stores and supermarkets. But it is advisable for someone interested in making Japanese and Korean food to stock up with some standard items, such as soy sauce – for Japanese dishes, make sure it is the Japanese variety — *mirin* (sweet

A family from the Ainu, an important sub-group from the northern archipelago of Japan.

cooking wine), *sake* (dry rice wine), *miso* paste and perhaps sesame oil. All can be kept for long periods, and can be obtained from Japanese food stores; some are stocked by general Oriental or Chinese stores.

The preparation of Japanese and Korean food is not as difficult as it might seem: the cutting of vegetables, particularly, is considered to be very important and something of an art form. There are no set rules for menus: but dishes are usually chosen to give variety in taste and colour. Remember that in Japanese and Korean meals the side dishes might not seem very substantial, but the volume is made up with rice; about half a cup of uncooked rice is usually allowed for each person.

Do not be afraid to vary the proportions of ingredients in the recipes which follow, or to adapt them to your own requirements. The important thing is to find the tastes which suit you best — and the recipes you enjoy most.

The face of Japan is delicate, beautiful and full of ceremony and grace.

SOUPS & NOODLES

Dashi

(Basic Stock)

Dashi is used extensively in Japanese cooking, and is the base for almost every soup and noodle dish. There are several types, but the simplest way to make it is with instant dashi powder (dashi-no-moto), which is obtainable from Japanese and some general Oriental stores. If all else fails, a chicken stock (bouillon) cube can be used as a substitute – although this does of course affect the authenticity (not to mention the taste) of the cooked dish.

Metric/Imperial	American
⅓ tsp. instant dashi powder (dashi-no-moto)	⅓ tsp. instant dashi powder (dashi-no-moto)
250ml./8fl.oz. water	1 cup water

Add the dashi powder to boiling water and set over moderately low heat. Boil for about 1 minute, stirring gently to blend. Remove from the heat and use as described in the various recipes.
Makes 250ml./8fl. oz. (1 cup) stock
Preparation and cooking time: 2 minutes

Kombo to Katsuobushi no Dashi

(Home-made Stock)

If you prefer to make your own dashi, the recipe which follows is one version. Kombo (dried kelp) and katsuobushi (dried bonito fish [tuna]) are essential ingredients and both can be bought in Japanese or Oriental stores, or in the case of kombu, in many health food stores. Kombu is sold in sheets and the katsuobushi either in flakes or in a solid block, which then has to be flaked.

Metric/Imperial	American
5cm./2in. piece of kombu	2in. piece of kombu
250ml./8fl.oz. water	1 cup water
1 tsp. katsuobushi	1 tsp. katsuobushi

Put the kombu and water into a small saucepan and bring to the boil, stirring constantly to release the flavour of the kelp. Remove from the heat and drain the water into a second saucepan, discarding the kombu pieces. Add the katsuobushi flakes and set the saucepan over moderate heat. Bring to the boil and boil for 1 minute. Remove the pan from the heat and set aside until the flakes settle. Strain the liquid, discarding the flakes.
The stock is now ready to use.
Makes 250ml./8fl.oz. (1 cup) stock
Preparation and cooking time: 5 minutes

Oysters fresh from the sea, still in the half shell. They can be used as a substitute for clams in the recipe given on this page.

Hamaguri Sumashi-Jiru

(Clam and Mushroom Soup)

Oysters can be substituted for the clams in this recipe. If used, omit the soaking period and add straight to the water.

Metric/Imperial	American
8 clams, soaked in salt water for 3 hours and drained	8 clams, soaked in salt water for 3 hours and drained
salt	salt
8 small button mushroom caps	8 small button mushroom caps
8 watercress sprigs	8 watercress sprigs
1 tsp. soya sauce	1 tsp. soy sauce
monosodium glutamate (optional)	MSG (optional)
125ml./4fl.oz. sake or dry sherry	½ cup sake or dry sherry
4 pieces of lemon rind	4 pieces of lemon rind

Put the clams and about 900ml./1½ pints (3¾ cups) of water into a large saucepan. Bring to the boil, then continue to boil until the shells open. Discard any that do not open. Remove any scum which rises to the surface and stir in salt to taste, the mushroom caps and watercress. Cook for 1 minute. Stir in soy sauce, mono-sodium glutamate to taste and the sake or sherry and return the soup to the boil.

Put one piece of lemon rind into each of four serving bowls, then divide the soup among the bowls. Serve at once.

Serves 4

Preparation and cooking time: 3¼ hours

Yakinasu no Miso Shiru

(Miso Soup with Fried Aubergine [Eggplant])

Metric/Imperial	American
125ml./4fl.oz. vegetable oil	½ cup vegetable oil
2 medium aubergines, sliced and dégorged	2 medium eggplants, sliced and dégorged
1.2l./2 pints dashi	5 cups dashi
4 Tbs. miso paste	4 Tbs. miso paste
2 mint leaves, thinly sliced	2 mint leaves, thinly sliced
mustard to taste	mustard to taste

Heat the oil in a frying-pan. When it is hot, add the aubergine (eggplant) slices and fry over moderately high heat until the skin begins to burn and peel. Remove from the heat and transfer the aubergines (eggplants) to a chopping board. Carefully peel off the skin and chop the flesh into bite-sized pieces. Divide the pieces among 4 to 6 soup bowls and keep hot.

Heat the dashi in a saucepan until it comes to the boil. Stir in the miso paste until it melts, forming a suspension in the liquid.

Pour the liquid over the aubergine (eggplant) pieces and add some mint leaf slices and mustard to taste to each bowl. Serve at once.

Serves 4–6

Preparation and cooking time: 35 minutes

Iwashi no Tsumire Jiru

(Clear Soup with Sardine Balls)

Metric/Imperial	American
5 fresh sardines, cleaned and with the heads removed	5 fresh sardines, cleaned and with the heads removed
2 Tbs. miso paste	2 Tbs. miso paste
1cm./½in. piece of fresh root ginger, peeled and grated	½in. piece of fresh green ginger, peeled and grated
1 Tbs. flour	1 Tbs. flour
1.2l./2 pints water	5 cups water
2 Tbs. soya sauce	2 Tbs. soy sauce
¼ tsp. salt	¼ tsp. salt
1 medium turnip, thinly sliced then quartered	1 medium turnip, thinly sliced then quartered
4 small pieces of lemon rind	4 small pieces of lemon rind

Remove the main bones from the sardines and clean them in salted water. Dry on kitchen towels and chop into small pieces. Put the sardines into a blender and blend until smooth. Alternatively, pound in a mortar with a pestle until smooth. Stir the miso paste, grated ginger and flour into the sardines and beat until they are thoroughly combined. Using the palm of your hands, gently roll small pieces of the mixture into balls.

Bring the water to the boil in a large saucepan. Drop in the fish balls and cook until they rise to the surface. Using a slotted spoon, transfer the fish balls to a plate and strain the liquid into a fresh pan. Stir in the soy sauce and salt.

In the meantime, cook the turnip in boiling water for about 5 minutes, or until the pieces are crisp. Drain and reserve.

Reheat the strained soup liquid and add the fish balls. Bring to the boil, then stir in the turnip.

Transfer to soup bowls and garnish with lemon rind.

Serves 4–6

Preparation and cooking time: 40 minutes

Tofu no Miso Shiru

(Bean Paste Soup with Bean Curd)

Metric/Imperial	American
1.2l./2 pints dashi	5 cups dashi
4 Tbs. miso paste	4 Tbs. miso paste
2 bean curd cakes (tofu), cut into small cubes	2 bean curd cakes (tofu), cut into small cubes
2 spring onions, finely chopped	2 scallions, finely chopped

Put the dashi into a large saucepan and set over moderate heat. Stir in the miso paste until it melts. Raise the heat to high and add the bean curd pieces. Boil until the bean curd rises to the surface of the liquid.

Serve at once, garnished with the spring onions (scallions).

Serves 4–6

Preparation and cooking time: 10 minutes

Kong-Na-Mool Kuk

(Bean Sprout Soup)   (Korea)

Metric/Imperial	American
225g./8oz. lean beef, cut into thin strips	8oz. lean beef, cut into thin strips
2 garlic cloves, crushed	2 garlic cloves, crushed
2 tsp. roasted sesame seeds, ground	2 tsp. roasted sesame seeds, ground
2 spring onions, green part only, finely chopped	2 scallions, green part only, finely chopped
salt and pepper	salt and pepper
3 Tbs. soya sauce	3 Tbs. soy sauce
1½ Tbs. sesame oil	1½ Tbs. sesame oil
700g./1½lb. bean sprouts	3 cups bean sprouts
1.751./3 pints water	1½ quarts water

Mix the beef, garlic, sesame seeds, half the spring onions (scallions), the salt and pepper and half the soy sauce together. Heat the oil in a saucepan. When it is hot, add the meat and stir-fry until it is evenly browned .Stir in the bean sprouts and stir-fry for a further 3 minutes.

   Pour in the water and remaining soy sauce and bring to the boil. Cover and simmer for 30 minutes. Stir in the remaining spring onion (scallion) and simmer for a further 5 minutes.

Serves 4–6
Preparation and cooking time: 40 minutes

Sumashi Jiru

(Chicken and Noodle Soup)

The type of noodle most commonly used in this soup is udon, *which somewhat resembles spaghetti in appearance. If* udon *is not available, then spaghetti vermicelli or any similar noodle may be substituted.*

Metric/Imperial	American
350g./12oz. udon	12oz. udon
1 large chicken breast, skinned, boned and cut into thin strips	1 large chicken breast, skinned, boned and cut into thin strips
1.21./2 pints dashi	5 cups dashi
6 dried mushrooms, soaked in cold water for 30 minutes, drained and sliced	6 dried mushrooms, soaked in cold water for 30 minutes, drained and sliced
2 tsp. soya sauce	2 tsp. soy sauce
2 spring onions, chopped	2 scallions, chopped
6 strips of lemon rind	6 strips of lemon rind

Cook the noodles in boiling salted water for 5 to 12 minutes, or until they are just tender. Drain and keep hot.

   Put the chicken meat strips into a large saucepan and pour over the dashi. Bring to the boil, then reduce the heat to moderate. Cook for 3 minutes. Add the mushrooms and soy sauce and cook for a further 2 minutes. Stir in the udon and return to the boil. Cook for 1 minute, then remove the pan from the heat.

Pour the soup either into a large warmed tureen, or into six individual small soup bowls. Garnish with spring onions (scallions) and lemon before serving.
Serves 6
Preparation and cooking time: 1 hour

Tofu no Ankake

(Bean Curd Soup)

Metric/Imperial	American
1.2 l./2 pints dashi	5 cups dashi
3 Tbs. soya sauce	3 Tbs. soy sauce
½ tsp. salt	½ tsp. salt
2 Tbs. mirin or sweet sherry	2 Tbs. mirin or sweet sherry
2 Tbs. cornflour, mixed to a paste with 2 Tbs. water	2 Tbs. cornstarch, mixed to a paste with 2 Tbs. water
2 Tbs. water	2 Tbs. water
4 dried mushrooms, soaked in cold water for 30 minutes, drained and sliced	4 dried mushrooms, soaked in cold water for 30 minutes, drained and sliced
350g./12oz. bean curd cakes (tofu), diced	2 cups diced bean curd cakes (tofu)
1cm./½in. piece of fresh root ginger, peeled and grated	½in. piece of fresh green ginger, peeled and grated

Put the dashi, soy sauce, salt, mirin or sherry, cornflour (cornstarch) mixture and mushrooms into a large saucepan and bring to the boil, stirring constantly. Reduce the heat to low, cover and simmer the soup for 15 minutes. Stir in the bean curd and simmer for a further 5 minutes.
   Ladle the soup into individual soup bowls, dividing the bean curd pieces equally among them. Garnish each bowl with a little grated ginger and serve.
Serves 4–6
Preparation and cooking time: 1 hour

Chawan Mushi

(Chicken and Steamed Vegetables in Egg)

Metric/Imperial	American
1 small chicken breast, boned and diced	1 small chicken breast, boned and diced
soya sauce	soy sauce
50g./2oz. firm white fish, skinned and cut into 4 pieces	2oz. firm white fish, skinned and cut into 4 pieces
salt	salt
8 prawns, shelled	8 shrimp, shelled
4 mushrooms caps, quartered	4 mushroom caps, quartered
50g./2oz. French beans, thinly sliced and parboiled	⅓ cup green beans, thinly sliced and parboiled
EGG MIXTURE	EGG MIXTURE
900ml./1½ pints dashi	3¾ cups dashi
1½ tsp. salt	1½ tsp. salt
1½ tsp. soya sauce	1½ tsp. soy sauce
monosodium glutamate (optional)	MSG (optional)
1 tsp. mirin or sweet sherry	1 tsp. mirin or sweet sherry
4 eggs, plus 2 egg yolks, lightly beaten	4 eggs, plus 2 egg yolks, lightly beaten

Tofu No Ankake (Bean Curd Soup) and Chawan Mushi (Chicken and Steamed Vegetables in Egg) are both served as soup courses in Japan – although Chawan Mushi is also a popular breakfast dish.

Sprinkle the chicken pieces with soy sauce and set aside for 5 minutes. Sprinkle the fish pieces with salt and set aside.

Meanwhile, to make the egg mixture, mix the dashi, salt, soy sauce, monosodium glutamate to taste and mirin or sherry together. Pour the beaten eggs slowly into the mixture, stirring gently. Set aside.

Divide the chicken dice, fish pieces, prawns or shrimp and mushrooms among four small ovenproof bowls. Pour the egg mixture on top and cover, leaving the covers slightly ajar.

Arrange the bowls in the top of a double boiler and half fill the bottom with boiling water. (If you do not have a double boiler, improvise by using a small baking dish set in a deep roasting pan. Fill the pan with water until it comes halfway up the sides of the baking dish.) Steam the mixture for 25 minutes, or until the eggs have set. (The surface should be yellow not brown and although the egg will be set on the outside it should still contain some liquid inside.)

About 5 minutes before the end of the cooking time, remove the covers from the bowls and garnish with the sliced beans. Serve hot, either as a soup course or as a breakfast dish.

Serves 4
Preparation and cooking time: $1\frac{1}{4}$ hours

Mandoo

(Meat Dumpling Soup)   (Korea)

Metric/Imperial	American
SOUP	SOUP
1.75 l./3 pints beef stock	7½ cups beef stock
2 Tbs. soya sauce	2 Tbs. soy sauce
1 Tbs. roasted sesame seeds, ground	1 Tbs. roasted sesame seeds, ground
1 large spring onion, chopped	1 large scallion, chopped
DUMPLING DOUGH	DUMPLING DOUGH
350g./12oz. flour	3 cups flour
250ml./8fl.oz. water	1 cup water
DUMPLING FILLING	DUMPLING FILLING
2 Tbs. vegetable oil	2 Tbs. vegetable oil
225g./8oz. minced beef	8oz. ground beef
1 onion, finely chopped	1 onion, finely chopped
1 garlic clove, crushed	1 garlic clove, crushed
50g./2oz. button mushrooms, chopped	½ cup chopped button mushrooms
225g./8oz. bean sprouts, chopped	1 cup chopped bean sprouts
2 spring onions, finely chopped	2 scallions, finely chopped
2 Tbs. soya sauce	2 Tbs. soy sauce
1 Tbs. roasted sesame seeds, ground	1 Tbs. roasted sesame seeds, ground
½ tsp. salt	½ tsp. salt

First make the dumpling dough. Put the flour into a mixing bowl and make a well in the centre. Gradually pour in the water, beating with a wooden spoon until the mixture forms a smooth dough. Turn the dough out on to a lightly floured board and knead for 5 minutes. Return to the bowl, cover with a damp cloth and set aside to 'rest' for 15 minutes while you prepare the filling.

Heat the oil in a frying-pan. When it is hot, add the beef, onion and garlic and fry for 5 minutes, stirring occasionally, or until the beef loses its pinkness. Stir in the mushrooms, bean sprouts, half the spring onions (scallions), soy sauce, sesame seeds and salt and bring to the boil. Cook for 1 minute, stirring frequently, then remove the pan from the heat.

To make the soup, pour the stock and soy sauce into a large saucepan and bring to the boil. Reduce the heat to moderately low and stir in the sesame seeds. Cook for 10 minutes.

Meanwhile, assemble the dumplings. Roll out the dough very thinly, then, using a 7.5cm./3in. pastry cutter, cut into circles. Spoon about 1 tablespoonful of filling on to the lower half of the circle, then fold over to make a semi-circle, pressing the edges firmly together so that the filling is completely enclosed.

Carefully add the dumplings to the soup and continue to cook until they come to the surface. Cook for 2 minutes longer, then transfer the mixture to a warmed tureen or ladle into individual soup bowls. Garnish the soup with the remaining chopped spring onion (scallion) before serving.

Serves 6–8

Preparation and cooking time: 45 minutes

Kitsune Donburi

('Fox' Noodles)

The unusual name of this dish (kitsune is the Japanese word for fox) comes about because, so folklore has it, the fox is very partial to bean curd which, with udon *noodles, is the main ingredient of the dish.* Udon *noodles greatly resemble spaghetti in shape and texture though they are lighter coloured – spaghetti, or even vermicelli or tagliatelle can therefore be substituted if Japanese-style noodles are not available.*

Metric/Imperial	American
BEAN CURD	BEAN CURD
175g./6oz. bean curd cakes (tofu), cut into six pieces	6oz. bean curd cakes (tofu), cut into six pieces
125ml./4fl.oz. dashi	½ cup dashi
75ml./3fl.oz. soya sauce	⅓ cup soy sauce
2 Tbs. mirin or sweet sherry	2 Tbs. mirin or sweet sherry
2 Tbs. sugar	2 Tbs. sugar
¼ tsp. monosodium glutamate (optional)	¼ tsp. MSG (optional)
NOODLES	NOODLES
1.2l./2 pints water	5 cups water
1 tsp. salt	1 tsp. salt
225g./8oz. udon	8oz. udon
KAKEJIRU SOUP	KAKEJIRU SOUP
1.2l./2 pints dashi	5 cups dashi
125ml./4fl.oz. soya sauce	½ cup soy sauce
125ml./4fl.oz. mirin or sweet sherry	½ cup mirin or sweet sherry
½ tsp. salt	½ tsp. salt
¼ tsp. monosodium glutamate	¼ tsp. MSG
2 spring onions, thinly sliced	2 scallions, thinly sliced

To make the bean curd, put the bean curd, dashi, soy sauce, mirin or sherry, sugar and monosodium glutamate into a saucepan and bring to the boil, stirring occasionally. Reduce the heat to low and simmer for 20 to 25 minutes, or until the bean curd has absorbed most of the liquid.

Meanwhile, prepare the noodles. Cook the udon in boiling, salted water for 10 to 12 minutes, or until they are just tender. Drain and return them to the saucepan. Set aside and keep hot.

To make the soup, put the dashi, soy sauce, mirin or sherry, salt, monosodium glutamate and spring onions *(scallions)* into a second large saucepan. Bring to the boil, reduce the heat to low and simmer the soup for 10 minutes.

To serve, divide the noodles between individual soup bowls. Place some bean curd on top and spoon over any remaining bean curd liquid. Pour over the soup, then serve at once.

Serves 6–8
Preparation and cooking time: 1 hour

Wu-Dung

(Fried Noodles)   (Korea)

Chinese rice noodles would probably be the most authentic type of pasta to use in this dish, but if they are unavailable, egg noodles or vermicelli can be substituted.

Metric/Imperial	American
350g./12oz. rice vermicelli	12oz. rice vermicelli
50ml./2fl.oz. vegetable oil	¼ cup vegetable oil
225g./8oz. rump steak, cut into strips	8oz. rump steak, cut into thin strips
3 spring onions, chopped	3 scallions, chopped
1 garlic clove, crushed	1 garlic clove, crushed
125g./4oz. button mushrooms, sliced	1 cup sliced button mushrooms
125g./4oz. peeled prawns	4oz. peeled shrimp
1 bean curd cake (tofu), chopped	1 bean curd cake (tofu), chopped
2 Tbs. soya sauce	2 Tbs. soy sauce
1 tsp. sugar	1 tsp. sugar
1 Tbs. roasted sesame seeds, ground	1 Tbs. roasted sesame seeds, ground

Cook the vermicelli in boiling, salted water for 5 minutes. Drain and keep warm.

Heat the oil in a large, deep frying-pan. When it is hot, add the steak strips and stir-fry until they lose their pinkness. Add the spring onions (scallions) and garlic to the pan and stir-fry for 2 minutes. Add the mushrooms, prawns (shrimp) and bean curd and stir-fry for a further 2 minutes. Add the soy sauce, sugar and sesame seeds, then stir in the vermicelli. Cook the mixture for a further 2 minutes, or until the vermicelli is heated through.

Transfer the mixture to a warmed serving bowl and serve at once.

Serves 4
Preparation and cooking time: 20 minutes

Hiyashi Somen

(Iced Noodles)

Metric/Imperial	American
450g./1lb. somen or noodles	1lb. somen or noodles
2 hard-boiled eggs, thinly sliced	2 hard-cooked eggs, thinly sliced
2 tomatoes, thinly sliced	2 tomatoes, thinly sliced
⅓ medium cucumber, peeled and cubed	⅓ medium cucumber, peeled and cubed
175g./6oz. lean cooked ham, cubed	1 cup lean cooked ham cubes
4 mint leaves, cut into strips	4 mint leaves, cut into strips

SAUCE	SAUCE
900ml./1½ pints dashi	3¾ cups dashi
150ml.5fl.oz. soya sauce	⅔ cup soy sauce
2 Tbs. sugar	2 Tbs. sugar
150ml./5fl.oz. sake or dry sherry	⅔ cup sake or dry sherry
monosodium glutamate (optional)	MSG (optional)
2 dried mushrooms, soaked in cold water for 30 minutes, drained and chopped	2 dried mushrooms, soaked in cold water for 30 minutes, drained and chopped

Cook the somen or noodles in boiling salted water for 5 minutes, or until they are just tender. Drain and rinse under cold running water. Transfer to a bowl and put into the refrigerator for 30 minutes.

Meanwhile, make the sauce. Put the dashi into a large saucepan and add all the remaining sauce ingredients. Bring to the boil and cook briskly for 8 minutes. Remove from the heat and set aside to cool.

Arrange the eggs, tomatoes, cucumber and ham decoratively on a large serving platter and sprinkle over the mint strips.

To serve, put the somen noodles over a bed of ice cubes, or sprinkle them with ice chips. Pour the sauce mixture into individual serving bowls. Traditionally, each guest helps himself to a portion of each dish, dipping the noodles into the sauce before eating.

Serves 6
Preparation and cooking time: 1¼ hours

Buta Udon

(Noodles with Pork)

Metric/Imperial	American
1.2l./2 pints dashi	5 cups dashi
275g./10oz. lean pork meat, cut into thin strips	10oz. lean pork meat, cut into thin strips
2 leeks, cleaned and cut into 2½cm./1in. lengths	2 leeks, cleaned and cut into 1in. lengths
150ml./5fl.oz. soya sauce	⅔ cup soy sauce
1½ Tbs. sugar	1½ Tbs. sugar
½ tsp. monosodium glutamate (optional)	½ tsp. MSG (optional)
salt	salt
350g./12oz. udon or spaghetti	12oz. udon or spaghetti
2 spring onions, finely chopped	2 scallions, finely chopped
paprika or hichimi togarashi	paprika or hichimi togarashi

Pour the dashi into a large saucepan and bring to the boil. Add the pork strips and leeks and cook the meat for 5 to 8 minutes, or until they are cooked through. Remove the pan from the heat and stir in the soy sauce, sugar and monosodium glutamate. Keep hot.

Meanwhile, cook the noodles in boiling salted water for 5 to 12 minutes, or until they are just tender. Drain and stir them into the soup. Return to moderate heat and bring to the boil.

To serve, divide the soup among 4 to 6 serving bowls and garnish with spring onions (scallions) and paprika or hichimi togarashi to taste.

Serve at once.

Serves 4–6
Preparation and cooking time: 30 minutes

RICE

Gohan

(Plain Boiled Rice, Japanese Style)

Short-grain rice is the closest Western equivalent to Japanese rice and has therefore been suggested here; long-grain can, of course, be substituted, but the texture will be a little different. The proportion of water to rice is always vital in rice cooking but it does tend to vary a little according to the age and quality of the rice grains. The amounts given below, therefore, are approximate and should be taken as a guide only. The finished product should be white, shiny, soft and moist; never wet and sticky.

Metric/Imperial	American
450g./1lb. short-grain rice	2⅔ cups short-grain rice
600ml./1 pint water	2½ cups water

Wash the rice to remove the starch, under cold running water. Alternatively, put the rice into a bowl, add water and stir and drain. Repeat two or three times until the water is almost clear.

Put the rice into a large, heavy saucepan and pour over the water. Bring to the boil, cover the pan and reduce the heat to low. Simmer for 15 to 20 minutes, or until the rice is cooked and the liquid absorbed. Reduce the heat to an absolute minimum and leave for 15 minutes. Turn off the heat but leave the saucepan on the burner for a further 10 minutes.

Transfer to a warmed serving bowl. The rice is now ready to serve.
Serves 4-6
Preparation and cooking time: 1 hour

Kuri Gohan

(Chestnut Rice)

Metric/Imperial	American
450g./1lb. short-grain rice	2⅔ cups short-grain rice
½kg./1lb. chestnuts	2⅔ cups chestnuts
900ml./1½ pints water	3¾ cups water
1½ Tbs. sake or dry sherry	1½ Tbs. sake or dry sherry
1 tsp. salt	1 tsp. salt

Wash the rice, then soak it for 1 hour.

Meanwhile, put the chestnuts into a saucepan and pour over the water. Bring to the boil, then parboil for 15 minutes. Drain and remove the skins from the chestnuts. Quarter them if they are large; keep them whole if they are not.

Add the chestnuts, sake or sherry and salt to the drained rice and cook, following the instructions given in *Gohan*.

Serve at once.
Serves 4-6
Preparation and cooking time: 1¾ hours
Note: You can cheat on this recipe by substituting a 450g./1lb. can of whole chestnuts for the fresh chestnuts above. In this case, the parboiling can be omitted and the chestnuts should be added straight to the rice.

Maze Gohan

(Mixed Vegetables and Rice)

Maze Gohan is a superb
mixture of rice, peas,
carrots, peas and shrimps,
delicately flavoured with
ginger, sake and
ginko nuts.

Metric/Imperial	American
1 large dried mushroom, soaked in cold water for 30 minutes, drained and finely chopped	1 large dried mushroom, soaked in cold water for 30 minutes, drained and finely chopped
2 carrots, sliced	2 carrots, sliced
2½cm./1in. piece of fresh root ginger, peeled and chopped	1in. piece of fresh green ginger, peeled and chopped
12 tinned ginko nuts, drained	12 canned ginko nuts, drained
2 celery stalks, chopped	2 celery stalks, chopped
2 Tbs. soya sauce	2 Tbs. soy sauce
1 Tbs. sake or dry sherry	1 Tbs. sake or dry sherry
½ tsp. salt	½ tsp. salt
700g./1½lb. short-grain rice, soaked in cold water for 1 hour and drained	4 cups short-grain rice, soaked in cold water for 1 hour and drained
900ml./1½ pints water	3¾ cups water
125g./4oz. green peas, weighed after shelling	½ cup green peas, weighed after shelling
125g./4oz. shelled shrimps	½ cup shelled shrimp

Put the mushroom, carrots, ginger, ginko nuts, celery, soy sauce, sake, salt and
rice into a large, heavy saucepan. Pour over the water and bring to the boil. Cover
the pan, reduce the heat to low and simmer the rice for 15 to 20 minutes, or until
it is cooked and the water absorbed.

Stir in the peas and shrimps and simmer for a further 10 minutes. (If the
mixture becomes a little dry during this period add a tablespoonful or two
of water.)

Transfer to a warmed serving dish and serve at once.

Serves 4
Preparation and cooking time: 1½ hours

Song i Pahb

(Rice and Mushrooms) (Korea)

Metric/Imperial	American
1 Tbs. sesame oil	1 Tbs. sesame oil
4 spring onions, chopped	4 scallions, chopped
225g./8oz. mushrooms, thinly sliced	2 cups thinly sliced mushrooms
175g./6oz. lean cooked meat, very finely chopped	1 cup very finely chopped lean cooked meat
2 Tbs. soya sauce	2 Tbs. soy sauce
2 tsp. roasted sesame seeds, ground	2 tsp. roasted sesame seeds, ground
salt and pepper	salt and pepper
350g./12oz. long-grain rice, soaked in cold water for 30 minutes and drained	2 cups long-grain rice, soaked in cold water for 30 minutes and drained
725ml./1¼ pints water	3 cups water

Heat the oil in a large frying-pan. When it is hot, stir in the spring onions (scallions), mushrooms, meat, soy sauce, sesame seeds and salt and pepper, and cook for 3 minutes, stirring constantly. Stir the mixture into the rice and transfer to a saucepan. Pour over the water and bring to the boil. Cover, reduce the heat to very low and simmer for 30 minutes, or until the rice is very dry and fluffy and the liquid completely absorbed; do not remove the lid during the cooking period.
Serves 4-6
Preparation and cooking time: 1 hour

Katsudon

(Pork Cutlets with Rice)

Metric/Imperial	American
450g./1lb. short-grain rice	2⅔ cups short-grain rice
600ml./1 pint water	2½ cups water
575g./1¼lb. pork fillet, cut into 4 cutlets	1¼lb. pork tenderloin, cut into 4 cutlets
4 eggs, lightly beaten	4 eggs, lightly beaten
50g./2oz. flour	½ cup flour
75g./3oz. dry breadcrumbs	1 cup dry breadcrumbs
vegetable oil for deep-frying	vegetable oil for deep-frying
650ml./1¼ pints dashi	3 cups dashi
150ml./5fl.oz. soya sauce	⅔ cup soy sauce
1½ Tbs. mirin or sweet sherry	1½ Tbs. mirin or sweet sherry
2 medium onions, thinly sliced into rings	2 medium onions, thinly sliced into rings

Cook the rice, following the instructions given in *Gohan*.

Meanwhile, coat the pork cutlets first in half the eggs, then in the flour and finally in the breadcrumbs, coating thoroughly and shaking off any excess.

Fill a large saucepan one-third full with oil and heat until it is very hot. Carefully lower the cutlets, two at a time, into the oil and fry until they are golden brown. Drain on kitchen towels. Set aside and keep hot.

Put the dashi, soy sauce and mirin into a pan and bring to the boil. Reduce the heat to low, add the onion rings and simmer for 10 minutes, or until the rings are soft. When the pork is cool enough to handle, slice into thin strips and add to the saucepan with the onion rings. Pour in the remaining beaten egg and simmer the mixture gently for 3 minutes. Remove from the heat.

Transfer the cooked rice into individual serving bowls. Top with the egg, onion and pork mixture and pour over any remaining liquid from the pan. Serve at once.

Serves 4
Preparation and cooking time: 50 minutes

Tendon

(Tempura with rice)

The 'tempura' offerings in Tendon always include fish and/or seafood but other than this, can be tailored to suit your taste and purse! The items listed below are therefore suggestions rather than ethnically essential.

Metric/Imperial	American
450g./1lb. short-grain rice	2⅔ cups short-grain rice
600ml./1 pint water	2½ cups water
TEMPURA	TEMPURA
4 large Dublin Bay prawns, shelled	4 large Gulf shrimp, shelled
3 small plaice fillets, quartered	3 small flounder fillets, quartered
1 red pepper, pith and seeds removed and cut into squares	1 red pepper, pith and seeds removed and cut into squares
6 button mushrooms	6 button mushrooms
50g./2oz. flour	½ cup flour
75ml./3fl.oz. water	⅓ cup water
1 small egg, lightly beaten	1 small egg, lightly beaten
vegetable oil for deep-frying	vegetable oil for deep-frying
SAUCE	SAUCE
175ml./6fl.oz. dashi	¾ cup dashi
3 Tbs. sake or dry sherry	3 Tbs. sake or dry sherry
3 Tbs. soya sauce	3 Tbs. soy sauce
½ tsp. sugar	½ tsp. sugar
monosodium glutamate (optional)	MSG (optional)
1cm./½in. piece of fresh root ginger, peeled and grated	½in. piece of fresh green ginger, peeled and grated
2 spring onions, chopped (to garnish)	2 scallions, chopped (to garnish)

Cook the rice, following the instructions given in *Gohan*.

Meanwhile, prepare the tempura. Arrange the seafood and vegetables on a platter. Beat the flour, water and egg together to make a light, thin batter, then dip the seafood and vegetable pieces into it to coat them thoroughly. Set aside.

Fill a large deep-frying pan about one-third full of vegetable oil and heat it until it is very hot. Carefully lower the seafood and vegetable pieces into the oil, a few at a time, and fry until they are crisp and golden brown. Using a slotted spoon, transfer the pieces to kitchen towels to drain, then keep hot while you prepare the sauce.

Put the dashi, sake or dry sherry, soy sauce, sugar and monosodium glutamate to taste into a saucepan and gently bring to the boil, stirring until the sugar has dissolved. Stir in the grated ginger and remove from the heat.

To serve, transfer the rice to a warmed serving bowl and arrange the tempura pieces decoratively over the top. Pour over the sauce and garnish with the chopped spring onions (scallions) before serving.

Serves 4-6
Preparation and cooking time: 1 hour

(See previous page) The translation of Mi-Iro Gohan is 'three-coloured rice'—so called because of the pretty pattern made by the three main ingredients, the rice, minced (ground) beef and green peas.

Mi-Iro Gohan

(Three-Coloured Rice)

Metric/Imperial	American
450g./1lb. short-grain rice	$2\frac{2}{3}$ cups short-grain rice
225g./8oz. green peas, weighed after shelling	1 cup green peas, weighed after shelling
MEAT	MEAT
275g./10oz. minced beef	10oz. ground beef
3 Tbs. soya sauce	3 Tbs. soy sauce
1 tsp. salt	1 tsp. salt
3 Tbs. sugar	3 Tbs. sugar
150ml./5fl.oz. dashi	$\frac{2}{3}$ cup dashi
4 Tbs. sake or dry sherry	4 Tbs. sake or dry sherry
EGGS	EGGS
5 eggs, lightly beaten	5 eggs, lightly beaten
1 Tbs. sugar	1 Tbs. sugar
1 Tbs. vegetable oil	1 Tbs. vegetable oil
$\frac{1}{4}$ tsp. salt	$\frac{1}{4}$ tsp. salt

Cook the rice, following the instructions given in *Gohan*.

Meanwhile, prepare the meat. Combine all the meat ingredients in a small saucepan and set over moderate heat. Cook, stirring constantly, until the meat loses its pinkness and is broken up into small grains. Cook for a further 5 minutes, or until the meat is cooked through. Remove from the heat and keep hot.

Beat all the egg ingredients together and put into a small saucepan. Set over low heat and cook, stirring constantly, until the eggs scramble and become dry. Remove from the heat and keep hot.

Cook the peas in boiling salted water for 5 minutes, or until they are just cooked. Remove from the heat, drain and set aside.

To assemble, fill individual serving bowls with rice. Level the top and arrange the meat mixture, egg mixture and peas decoratively on top, in three sections. Pour over any juices from the meat bowl and serve at once.

Serves 4-6
Preparation and cooking time: 1 hour

Iwashi no Kabayaki

(Sardines with Rice)

Metric/Imperial	American
450g./1lb. short-grain rice, soaked in cold water for 1 hour and drained	$2\frac{2}{3}$ cups short-grain rice, soaked in cold water for 1 hour and drained
12 sardines, cleaned, gutted and with the head removed	12 sardines, cleaned, gutted and with the head removed
3 Tbs. soya sauce	3 Tbs. soy sauce
4cm./1½in. piece of fresh root ginger, peeled and grated	1½in. piece of fresh green ginger, peeled and grated
50g./2oz. cornflour	½ cup cornstarch
50ml./2fl.oz. vegetable oil	¼ cup vegetable oil
225g./8oz. cooked green peas, weighed after shelling	1 cup cooked green peas, weighed after shelling

SAUCE

150ml./5fl.oz. soya sauce	$\frac{2}{3}$ cup soy sauce
4 Tbs. mirin or sweet sherry	4 Tbs. mirin or sweet sherry
2 Tbs. sugar	2 Tbs. sugar
3 Tbs. water	3 Tbs. water
monosodium glutamate (optional)	MSG (optional)
2 tsp. miso paste	2 tsp. miso paste

Cook the rice, following the instructions given in Gohan.

Meanwhile, remove the main bones from the sardines and splay open. Wash in lightly salted water then transfer to a shallow dish. Pour over the soy sauce and ginger and set aside at room temperature for 20 minutes, turning the fish from time to time. Remove the fish from the marinade and pat dry with kitchen towels.

Dip the fish in the cornflour (cornstarch), shaking off any excess. Heat the oil in a large frying-pan. When it is hot, add the sardines, in batches, and fry for 6 to 8 minutes or until they are golden and the flesh flakes.

Meanwhile, combine all the sauce ingredients, except the miso paste, and bring to the boil. Stir in the miso paste and continue cooking until it melts. Remove from the heat.

Pour off the oil from the sardines and add the sauce mixture. Bring to the boil then remove from the heat.

When the rice is cooked, arrange in deep serving bowls and top with the sardines. Pour over the soy sauce mixture and garnish with cooked green peas. Serve at once.

Serves 4
Preparation and cooking time: $1\frac{3}{4}$ hours

Nigiri Zushi

(Rice and Fish 'Sandwiches')

Metric/Imperial	American
700g./1½lb. short-grain rice	4 cups short-grain rice
8 large prawns, in the shell	8 large shrimp, in the shell
1 lemon sole fillet, skinned	1 lemon sole fillet, skinned
1 mackerel fillet, skinned	1 mackerel fillet; skinned
40g./1½oz. smoked salmon	$\frac{1}{6}$ cup smoked salmon
1 medium squid, cleaned, skinned and boned	1 medium squid, cleaned, skinned and boned
3 tsp. green horseraish (wasabi), mixed to a paste with 1 Tbs. water	3 tsp. green horseradish (wasabi), mixed to a paste with 1 Tbs. water
parsley or mint	parsley or mint
350ml./12fl.oz. soy sauce	1½ cups soy sauce
VINEGAR SAUCE	VINEGAR SAUCE
125ml./4fl.oz. white wine vinegar	½ cup white wine vinegar
1½ Tbs. sugar	1½ Tbs. sugar
1½ tsp. salt	1½ tsp. salt
monosodium glutamate (optional)	MSG (optional)

Cook the rice, following the instructions given in Gohan. Transfer the drained rice to a warmed bowl and set aside. To make the vinegar sauce, combine the vinegar, sugar, salt and monosodium glutamate to taste, then pour the mixture over the rice. Stir gently with a wooden spoon and set aside to cool at room temperature.

Cook the prawns (shrimp) in boiling water until they turn pink. Drain and

29

remove the shell and heads. Gently cut along the underside of the prawns (shrimp) and splay them open. Set aside. Sprinkle the sole with salt, then neatly cut the flesh into rectangles about 5cm by 2½cm./2in. by 1in. and just under 1cm./½in. thick. Cut the mackerel, smoked salmon and boned squid into pieces about the same size as the sole.

Using the palm of your hand, gently shape about 1 tablespoon of the rice mixture into a wedge, about the size of your thumb. Smear a small amount of horseradish paste on to the middle of one piece of fish and press the fish and rice gently together to form a 'sandwich', with the horseradish in the centre. Continue this procedure, using up the remaining fish pieces and the remaining rice, but omitting the horseradish mixture for the prawns (shrimp). (You will probably find that the rice will stick to your hands slightly, so rinse them regularly in a bowl of water to which a dash of vinegar has been added.)

When the 'sandwiches' have been made, arrange them decoratively on a large flat dish and garnish with parsley or mint. Pour the soy sauce into individual small dipping bowls, and dip the 'sandwiches' into the soy sauce before eating. This is usually served as a snack or hors d'oeuvre in Japan.

Serves 6-8
Preparation and cooking time: 1 hour

Sashimi Gohan

(Prepared Fish and Rice)

Metric/Imperial	American
1 large mackerel, cleaned, gutted, then filleted	1 large mackerel, cleaned, gutted, then filleted
1 tsp. salt	1 tsp. salt
450ml./15fl.oz. white wine vinegar	2 cups white wine vinegar
350g./12oz. short-grain rice, soaked in cold water for 1 hour and drained	2 cups short-grain rice, soaked in cold water for 1 hour and drained
600ml./1 pint water	2½ cups water
GARNISH	GARNISH
4cm./1½in. piece of fresh root ginger, peeled and grated	1½in. piece of fresh green ginger, peeled and grated
5 spring onions, finely chopped	5 scallions, finely chopped
350ml./12fl.oz. soya sauce	1½ cups soy sauce
2 tsp. green horseradish (wasabi), mixed to a paste with 2 tsp. water	2 tsp. green horseradish (wasabi), mixed to a paste with 2 tsp. water

Sprinkle the mackerel fillets with salt and put into the refrigerator to chill for 1 hour. Remove from the refrigerator and soak in the vinegar for a further 1 hour.

Meanwhile, put the rice into a saucepan and cover with the water. Bring to the boil, reduce the heat to low and cover the pan. Simmer for 15 to 20 minutes, or until the rice is cooked and the water absorbed. Remove from the heat and transfer to a warmed serving bowl. Set aside and keep hot.

Remove the fish from the vinegar and pat dry with kitchen towels. Cut vertically into 1cm./½in. pieces, removing any bones. Arrange the fish decoratively on a serving dish and surround with the grated ginger and spring onions (scallions). Pour the soy sauce into small, individual dipping bowls and serve individual portions of the horseradish mixture.

To eat, mix horseradish to taste into the soy sauce and dip the mackerel pieces into the sauce before eating with the rice.

Serves 4
Preparation and cooking time: 2½ hours

Sashimi Gohan (Sliced Raw Fish with Rice) is so popular in Japan that there are restuarants devoted exclusively to preparing it. This version is simplicity itself, and the result is guaranteed to make a convert of even the most doubtful eater of uncooked fish!

31

Seki Han

(Red Cooked Rice)

This special festival dish is most authentic when the small red Japanese azuki beans are used. They can be obtained from many health food stores and oriental delicatessens. However, if they are not available, dried red kidney beans can be substituted successfully.

Metric/Imperial	American
275g./10oz. dried azuki beans, soaked overnight in cold water	1½ cups dried azuki beans, soaked overnight in cold water
350g./12oz. short-grain rice	2 cups short-grain rice
1 tsp. salt	1 tsp. salt
2 Tbs. sake or dry sherry	2 Tbs. sake or dry sherry
1 Tbs. soya sauce	1 Tbs. soy sauce

Put the beans and their soaking liquid into a saucepan and bring to the boil (top up with water if necessary, so that the beans are completely covered). Cover the pan, reduce the heat to low and cook the beans for 1 hour, or until they are just tender. Remove the pan from the heat and drain and reserve the bean cooking liquid. Transfer the beans to a bowl and set aside and keep hot.

Cook the rice, following the instructions given in *Gohan*, except that instead of using all water to cook the rice, use the bean cooking liquid and make up any extra liquid needed with water.

About 5 minutes before the rice is ready to serve, stir in the reserved beans, the salt, sake or sherry and soy sauce and cook until they are all heated through.

Transfer the mixture to a warmed serving bowl and serve at once.
Serves 3-4
Preparation and cooking time: 14 hours

Nori Maki

(Rice Rolls Wrapped in Seaweed)

Metric/Imperial	American
900g./2lb. short-grain rice	5⅓ cups short-grain rice
1.2l./2 pints water	5 cups water
¼ large mackerel, filleted	¼ large mackerel, filleted
150ml./5fl.oz. white wine vinegar	⅔ cup white wine vinegar
1 Tbs. kanpyo, soaked in cold salted water for 1 hour and drained	1 Tbs. kanpyo, soaked in cold salted water for 1 hour and drained
1 Tbs. soya sauce	1 Tbs. soy sauce
50ml./2fl.oz. water	¼ cup water
2 tsp. sugar	2 tsp. sugar
½ cucumber	½ cucumber
125g./4oz. fresh tuna fish	4oz. fresh tuna fish
4 sheets of nori (seaweed)	4 sheets of nori (seaweed)
3 tsp. green horseradish (wasabi), mixed to a paste with 1 Tbs. water	3 tsp. green horseradish (wasabi), mixed to a paste with 1 Tbs. water
350ml./12fl.oz. soya sauce	1½ cups soy sauce

VINEGAR SAUCE	VINEGAR SAUCE
125ml./4fl.oz. white wine vinegar	½ cup white wine vinegar
1½ Tbs. sugar	1½ Tbs. sugar
1½ tsp. salt	1½ tsp. salt
monosodium glutamate (optional)	MSG (optional)

Cook the rice, following the instructions given in *Gohan*. Transfer the drained rice to a warmed bowl and set aside. To make the vinegar sauce, combine the vinegar, sugar, salt and monosodium glutamate to taste, then pour the mixture over the rice. Stir gently with a wooden spoon and set aside to cool at room temperature.

Meanwhile, soak the mackerel in the vinegar for 1 hour. Put the kanpyo into a saucepan and just cover with water. Bring to the boil and cook briskly until it is just tender. Drain then return the kanpyo to the saucepan and add the soy sauce, water, and sugar. Cook over moderate heat for 10 minutes, to ensure that the flavours are absorbed into the kanpyo. Set aside.

Remove the mackerel from the vinegar and pat dry on kitchen towels. Cut the flesh vertically into long strips. Slice the cucumber and tuna fish into long thin strips, about the same length as the nori. Set aside.

Preheat the grill (broiler) to moderately high. Place the nori sheets on the rack and grill (broil) until it is crisp on one side. Remove from the heat and cut each sheet into half.

Place one half nori sheet on a flexible bamboo mat or heavy cloth napkin. Spread a handful of sushi rice over the top of the nori, to within about 5cm./2in. of all the edges. Smear a little horseradish over the sushi. Arrange two or three strands of mackerel across the centre of the rice and roll up the mat or napkin gently but firmly so that the mixture will stick together and form a long cylinder. Remove the mat and, in the same way, make cylinders of the remaining nori, sushi rice and fish. Omit the horseradish from the kanpyo mixture.

When all the cylinders have been formed, gently slice across them to form sections about 2½cm./1in. wide.

Pour the soy sauce into small individual dipping bowls and dip the nori sections into the sauce before eating.

Serve the nori maki either on its own as an hors d'oeuvre or as a light snack, or with nigiri zushi as a light meal.
Serves 8
Preparation and cooking time: 2½ hours

Chirashi Zushi

(Rice Salad with Fish)

Metric/Imperial	American
125g./4oz. French beans, sliced	⅔ cup sliced green beans
2 sheets of nori (seaweed)	2 sheets of nori (seaweed)
sprinkling of shredded ginger	sprinkling of shredded ginger
MACKEREL	MACKEREL
1 small mackerel, filleted	1 small mackerel, filleted
1 Tbs. salt	1 Tbs. salt
450ml./15fl.oz. white wine vinegar	2 cups white wine vinegar
RICE	RICE
450g./1lb. short-grain rice, soaked in cold water for 1 hour and drained	2⅔ cups short-grain rice, soaked in cold water for 1 hour and drained

Metric	Imperial/US
75ml./3fl.oz. white wine vinegar	⅓ cup white wine vinegar
1½ Tbs. sugar	1½ Tbs. sugar
1 Tbs. salt	1 Tbs. salt
KANPYO	KANPYO
handful of kanpyo, soaked in cold, salted water for 1 hour and drained	handful of kanpyo, soaked in cold, salted water for 1 hour and drained
3 Tbs. soya sauce	3 Tbs. soy sauce
2 Tbs. sugar	2 Tbs. sugar
250ml./8fl.oz. water	1 cup water
MUSHROOMS	MUSHROOMS
5 dried mushrooms, soaked in 450ml./15fl.oz. cold water for 30 minutes, stalks removed and caps sliced	5 dried mushrooms, soaked in 2 cups cold water for 30 minutes, stalks removed and caps sliced
1½ Tbs. soya sauce	1½ Tbs. soy sauce
3 Tbs. sugar	3 Tbs. sugar
1½ Tbs. sake or dry sherry	1½ Tbs. sake or dry sherry
½ tsp. salt	½ tsp. salt
CARROTS	CARROTS
1 large carrot, sliced	1 large carrot, sliced
2 tsp. sugar	2 tsp. sugar
¼ tsp. salt	¼ tsp. salt
EGGS	EGGS
3 eggs, lightly beaten	3 eggs, lightly beaten
few drops soya sauce	few drops soy sauce
½ tsp. salt	½ tsp. salt
½ Tbs. vegetable oil	2 Tbs. vegetable oil

Sprinkle the mackerel fillets with salt and put into the refrigerator to chill for 1 hour. Remove from the refrigerator and soak in the vinegar for a further 1 hour.

Cook the rice, following the instructions given in *Gohan*. Transfer the drained rice to a warm bowl and set aside. To make the vinegar sauce, combine the vinegar, sugar and salt, then pour the mixture over the rice. Stir gently with a wooden spoon and set aside to cool at room temperature.

Put the kanpyo into a saucepan and just cover with water. Bring to the boil and cook briskly until it is just tender. Drain, then return to the saucepan with the soy sauce, sugar and water. Cook over moderate heat for 10 minutes, to ensure that the flavours are absorbed into the kanpyo. Set aside.

Reserve the mushroom draining liquid and add to a small saucepan with the soy sauce, sugar, sake or sherry and salt. Stir in the mushroom pieces and bring to the boil. Cook over moderate heat for 15 minutes, then transfer the mushrooms to a plate with a slotted spoon. Add the carrots to the saucepan, with the sugar and salt. Reduce the heat to low and simmer until all of the sauce has evaporated. Remove from the heat and set aside.

Beat the eggs, soy sauce and salt together. Heat a little of the oil in a small frying-pan. When it is hot, add some of the egg mixture and fry until it forms a wafer-thin pancake. Using a spatula, carefully remove from the pan. Continue to cook the egg mixture in this way until it is all used up. When all the pancakes are cooked, roll them up together and slice them into thin strips. Set aside.

Cook the beans in boiling salted water for 5 minutes, or until they are just tender. Drain and set aside.

Remove the mackerel fillets from the vinegar and pat dry on kitchen towels. Cut vertically into thin strips and set aside.

Preheat the grill (broiler) to moderately high. Place the nori sheets on the rack and grill (broil) until crisp on both sides. Remove from the heat and set aside.

To assemble, arrange the rice in a large serving bowl. Combine the mushrooms, carrots and kanpyo and stir gently into the rice. Arrange the beans, eggs and sliced mackerel on top and sprinkle over the ginger. Crumble over the nori and serve at once.

Serves 4-6

Preparation and cooking time: 2¾ hours

Zushi rice (rice mixed with vinegar and sugar) forms the basis of Chirashi Zushi. It is garnished with nori, *a type of seaweed popular in Japan.*

Oyako Donburi

(Chicken and Eggs with Rice)

Metric/Imperial	American
450g./1lb. short-grain rice, soaked in cold water for 1 hour and drained	2⅔ cups short-grain rice, soaked in cold water for 1 hour and drained
3 Tbs. vegetable oil	3 Tbs. vegetable oil
2 small chicken breasts, skinned, boned and cut into thin strips	2 small chicken breasts, skinned, boned and cut into thin strips
2 medium onions, thinly sliced	2 medium onions, thinly sliced
4 eggs, lightly beaten	4 eggs, lightly beaten
2 sheets of nori (seaweed)	2 sheets of nori (seaweed)
SAUCE	SAUCE
4 Tbs. water	4 Tbs. water
4 Tbs. soya sauce	4 Tbs. soy sauce
4 Tbs. dashi	4 Tbs. dashi

Cook the rice, following the instructions given in *Gohan*.

Meanwhile, heat the oil in a frying-pan. When it is hot, add the chicken pieces and fry until they are just cooked through. Remove from the heat and, using a slotted spoon, transfer to a plate.

Combine the sauce ingredients together.

Put about a quarter of the sauce mixture into a small frying-pan and bring to the boil. Add about a quarter of the onions and fry briskly for 3 minutes. Add quarter of the chicken slices and quarter of the eggs. Reduce the heat to low and stir once. Leave until the egg has set then cover the pan and steam for 1 minute.

Spoon about a quarter of the rice into an individual serving bowl and top with the egg mixture. Repeat this process three more times, using up the remaining ingredients.

Meanwhile, preheat the grill (broiler) to moderately high. Place the nori on the rack of the grill (broiler) pan and grill (broil) until it is crisp. Remove from the heat and crumble over the rice and egg mixture. Serve at once.

Serves 4

Preparation and cooking time: 1¾ hours

Oboro

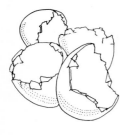

(Chicken and Rice)

Metric/Imperial	American
450g./1lb. short-grain rice	2⅔ cups short-grain rice
6 dried mushrooms, soaked in cold water for 30 minutes and drained	6 dried mushrooms, soaked in cold water for 30 minutes and drained
75ml./3fl.oz. soya sauce	⅓ cup soy sauce
75ml./3fl.oz. sake or dry sherry	⅓ cup sake or dry sherry
1 tsp. sugar	1 tsp. sugar
2 chicken breasts, skinned, boned and cut into strips	2 chicken breasts, skinned, boned and cut into strips
225./8oz. frozen green peas	1 cup frozen green peas
50ml./2fl.oz. vegetable oil	¼ cup vegetable oil
2 eggs, beaten	2 eggs, beaten

Cook the rice, following the instructions given in *Gohan*.

Remove the stalks from the mushrooms and cook the caps in boiling water for 5 minutes, drain then cut into slices. Set aside.

Put the soy sauce, sake or sherry and sugar into a large saucepan and bring to the boil, stirring constantly until the sugar has dissolved. Add the chicken strips and peas to the pan and reduce the heat to low. Cover and simmer for 5 minutes, or until the chicken strips are cooked. Remove from the heat and set aside.

Heat the oil in a small frying-pan. When it is hot, add the eggs and cook for 2 minutes, or until the bottom has set and is browned. Turn over the omelet and cook for 2 minutes on the other side. Slide the omelet on to a plate and cut into strips. Set aside.

When the rice is cooked, transfer it to a warmed serving bowl. Arrange the chicken strips and peas on top and pour over the chicken cooking liquid. Scatter over the mushrooms and omelet strips and serve at once.

Serves 4–6
Preparation and cooking time: 1 hour

Gyu Donburi

(Beef on Rice)

Metric/Imperial	American
450g./1lb. short-grain rice, soaked in cold water for 1 hour and drained	2⅔ cups short-grain rice, soaked in cold water for 1 hour and drained
175ml./6fl.oz. soya sauce	¾ cup soy sauce
175ml./6fl.oz. dashi	¾ cup dashi
3 Tbs. sugar	3 Tbs. sugar
½kg./1lb. rump steak, thinly sliced	1lb. rump steak, thinly sliced
50ml./2fl.oz. vegetable oil	¼ cup vegetable oil
2 green peppers, pith and seeds removed and cut into bite-sized pieces	2 green peppers, pith and seeds removed and cut into bite-sized pieces
½kg./1lb. leeks, cleaned and cut diagonally into 1cm./½in. lengths	1lb. leeks, cleaned and cut diagonally into ½in. lengths
4cm./1½in. piece of fresh root ginger, peeled and grated	1½in. piece of fresh green ginger, peeled and grated

Cook the rice, following the instructions given in *Gohan*.

Meanwhile, combine the soy sauce, dashi and sugar together in a large shallow dish. Add the beef slices and set aside to marinate at room temperature for 15 minutes, basting occasionally. Remove from the marinade and pat dry with kitchen towels. Reserve the marinade.

Heat half the oil in a large frying-pan. When it is hot, add the beef slices and cook for 2 minutes on each side. Reduce the heat to moderately low and cook for a further 2 minutes on each side. Stir in the reserved marinade and remove from the heat. Keep hot.

Heat the remaining oil in a second frying-pan. When it is hot, add the peppers and leeks and fry gently for 8 to 10 minutes, or until they are just cooked. Remove from the heat and set aside.

When the rice is cooked, transfer it to individual serving bowls. Either cut the beef into thin strips or serve it as it is. Arrange the peppers and leeks and beef to make three sections on top of the rice. Pour over the meat cooking juices and sprinkle with grated ginger.

Serve at once.

Serves 4
Preparation and cooking time: 1 hour

MEAT & POULTRY

Kushi Dango

(Meatballs)

Metric/Imperial	American
575g./1¼lb. minced beef	1¼lb. ground beef
4 spring onions, finely chopped	4 scallions, finely chopped
4cm./1½in. piece of fresh root ginger, peeled and grated	1½in. piece of fresh green ginger, peeled and grated
3 Tbs. flour	3 Tbs. flour
1 Tbs. soya sauce	1 Tbs. soy sauce
3 eggs, lightly beaten	3 eggs, lightly beaten
monosodium glutamate (optional)	MSG (optional)
vegetable oil for deep-frying	vegetable oil for deep-frying

Combine the beef, spring onions (scallions), ginger, flour, soy sauce, eggs and monosodium glutamate to taste in a large bowl. Using the palm of your hands, gently shape the mixture into small balls, about 2½cm./1in. in diameter.

Fill a large deep-frying pan about one-third full with vegetable oil and heat it until it is very hot. Carefully lower the meatballs, a few at a time, into the hot oil and fry until they are golden brown. Using a slotted spoon, remove the meatballs from the pan and drain on kitchen towels. Keep hot while you fry the remaining meatballs in the same way.

To serve, thread three or four meatballs each on to short skewers and serve as an hors d'oeuvre.

Serves 4–6
Preparation and cooking time: 40 minutes

San Juhk

(Beef Kebabs)   (Korea)

Metric/Imperial	American
½kg./1lb. rump steak, cut into 5cm./2in. strips	1lb. rump steak, cut into 2in. strips
1 green pepper, pith and seeds removed and cut into strips	1 green pepper, pith and seeds removed and cut into strips
4 spring onions, cut into 2½cm./1in. lengths	4 scallions, cut into 1in. lengths
2 eggs, beaten	2 eggs, beaten
50g./2oz. flour	½ cup flour
125ml./4fl.oz. vegetable oil	½ cup vegetable oil
MARINADE	MARINADE
2 Tbs. soya sauce	2 Tbs. soy sauce
1 Tbs. sesame oil	1 Tbs. sesame oil
1 garlic clove, crushed	1 garlic clove, crushed
1 tsp. sugar	1 tsp. sugar
1 Tbs. roasted sesame seeds, ground	1 Tbs. roasted sesame seeds, ground

First, make the marinade. Put the soy sauce, sesame oil, garlic clove, sugar and half the ground sesame seeds into a large, shallow bowl. Add the beef strips to the bowl and turn to baste thoroughly. Set aside at room temperature for 30 minutes. Remove the strips from the bowl and pat dry with kitchen towels. Discard the marinade.

Thread the beef on to skewers, alternating them with the pepper and spring onion (scallion) pieces. Carefully dip the skewers into the beaten eggs, then coat in the flour, shaking off any excess.

Heat the oil in a large frying-pan. When it is hot, carefully arrange the skewers in the pan. Fry, turning the skewers occasionally, for 8 to 10 minutes, or until the beef is brown and crisp. Remove from the heat and drain on kitchen towels.

Transfer the skewers to a warmed serving dish, sprinkle over the remaining sesame seeds and serve at once.

Serves 4
Preparation and cooking time: 1 hour

Gyuniku no Amiyaki

(Steak Marinated in Sesame)

Metric/Imperial	American
4 x 225g./8oz. rump steaks	4 x 8oz. rump steaks
MARINADE	MARINADE
1½ Tbs. sesame seeds	1½ Tbs. sesame seeds
1 garlic clove, crushed	1 garlic clove, crushed
1½ Tbs. soya sauce	1½ Tbs. soy sauce
1 Tbs. sake or dry sherry	1 Tbs. sake or dry sherry
1 tsp. sugar	1 tsp. sugar
DIPPING SAUCE	DIPPING SAUCE
2 spring onions, finely chopped	2 scallions, finely chopped
4cm./1½in. piece of fresh root ginger, peeled and grated	1½in. piece of fresh green ginger, peeled and grated
½ tsp. paprika or hichimi togarashi	½ tsp. paprika or hichimi togarashi
150ml./5fl.oz. soya sauce	⅔ cup soy sauce
2 Tbs. dashi	2 Tbs. dashi

First make the marinade. Fry the sesame seeds gently in a small frying-pan until they begin to 'pop'. Transfer them to a mortar and crush with a pestle to release the oil. Put the crushed seeds into a large shallow bowl and mix thoroughly with all the remaining marinade ingredients. Add the steaks to the dish and baste thoroughly. Set aside to marinate at room temperature for 30 minutes, turning the steaks and basting them occasionally.

Meanwhile, prepare the dipping sauce by mixing all the ingredients together. Pour the sauce into individual dipping bowls and set aside.

Preheat the grill (broiler) to moderately high.

Remove the steaks from the marinade and arrange on the rack of the grill (broiler). Grill (broil) for 2 minutes on each side, then reduce the heat to moderate. Grill (broil) for a further 2 minutes on each side for rare steaks; double the cooking time for medium.

Remove the steaks from the heat, transfer to a chopping board and carefully cut into strips. Arrange the strips on individual serving plates. Serve at once, with the dipping sauce.

Serves 4
Preparation and cooking time: 1 hour

Bul-Ko-Kee

(Barbecued Beef)   (Korea)

Metric/Imperial	American
½kg./1lb. topside of beef, very thinly sliced into strips	1lb. top round of beef, very thinly sliced into strips
3 Tbs. soft brown sugar	3 Tbs. soft brown sugar
125ml./4fl.oz. soya sauce	½ cup soy sauce
salt and pepper	salt and pepper
5 Tbs. roasted sesame seeds, ground	5 Tbs. roasted sesame seeds, ground
50ml./2fl.oz. sesame oil	4 Tbs. sesame oil
1 garlic clove, crushed	1 garlic clove, crushed
2 spring onions, green part only, finely chopped	2 scallions, green part only, finely chopped
½ tsp. monosodium glutamate (optional)	½ tsp. MSG (optional)

Mix the beef, sugar, soy sauce, salt and pepper to taste, half the sesame seeds, the oil, garlic, spring onions (scallions) and monosodium glutamate together. Set aside at room temperature for 2 hours, basting and turning the meat from time to time.

Preheat the grill (broiler) to hot.

Lay the beef strips on the lined grill (broiler) pan and grill (broil) for 5 to 8 minutes, or until the strips are cooked through and evenly browned. (If you prefer, the beef can be fried quickly in a little sesame oil until browned.)

Remove from the heat, sprinkle over the remaining sesame seeds and serve at once.

Serves 4
Preparation and cooking time: about 2¼ hours

Bul-Ko-Kee, a succulent mixture of beef strips, first marinated then barbecued and sprinkled with sesame seeds, is almost the Korean national dish. It is served here with Kim Chee, a popular Korean version of pickled cabbage.

Yuk-Kae-Jang-Kuk

(Beef Stew with Peppers)   (Korea)

Metric/Imperial	American
1kg./2lb. braising steak, cut into thin strips	2lb. chuck steak, cut into thin strips
3 green peppers, pith and seeds removed and cut into strips	3 green peppers, pith and seeds removed and cut into strips
3 red peppers, pith and seeds removed and cut into strips	3 red peppers, pith and seeds removed and cut into strips
3 spring onions, chopped	3 scallions, chopped
½ tsp. sugar	½ tsp. sugar
½ tsp. salt	½ tsp. salt
125ml./4fl.oz. soya sauce	½ cup soy sauce
175ml./6fl.oz. water	¾ cup water

Put all the ingredients into a heavy-bottomed saucepan and bring to the boil. Cover and simmer for 2 to 2½ hours, or until the beef is very tender. (Do not add any more liquid – enough is produced by the ingredients.)

Transfer to a warmed serving dish before serving.

Serves 4–6
Preparation and cooking time: 3 hours

Gyuniku no Kushiyaki

(Beef Kebabs with Green Pepper)

This dish is a sort of Japanese shashlik and the 'extra' fillings can be varied according to taste. The combination used here is particularly colourful, but you could substitute small whole onions, tomatoes, or mushrooms if you prefer.

Metric/Imperial	American
½kg./1lb. rump steak, cut into bite-sized cubes	1lb. rump steak, cut into bite -sized cubes
1 large green pepper, pith and seeds removed and cut into pieces about the same size as the meat cubes	1 large green pepper, pith and seeds removed and cut into pieces about the same size as the meat cubes
1 large red pepper, pith and seeds removed and cut into pieces about the same size as the meat cubes	1 large red pepper, pith and seeds removed and cut into pieces about the same size as the meat cubes
50g./2oz. flour	½ cup flour
2 eggs, beaten	2 eggs, beaten
75g./3oz. fine dry breadcrumbs	1 cup fine dry breadcrumbs
vegetable oil for deep-frying	vegetable oil for deep-frying
MARINADE	MARINADE
75ml./3fl.oz. soya sauce	⅓ cup soy sauce
3 Tbs. mirin or sweet sherry	3 Tbs. mirin or sweet sherry
2 spring onions, chopped	2 scallions, chopped
1 tsp. sugar	1 tsp. sugar
½ tsp. hichimi togarishi or paprika	½ tsp. hichimi togarishi or paprika

First, make the marinade. Put all the ingredients into a large, shallow dish and mix until they are thoroughly blended.

Thread the meat and pepper pieces on to skewers then arrange them carefully in the marinade mixture. Set aside at room temperature for at least 1 hour, turning the skewers from time to time so that all sides of the mixture become coated in the marinade. Remove from the marinade, then discard the marinade. Pat the cubes dry with kitchen towels and dip lightly in the flour, shaking off any excess. Dip the skewers into the beaten eggs, then coat thoroughly with the breadcrumbs, shaking off any excess.

Fill a large deep-frying pan about one-third full with vegetable oil and heat until it is very hot. Carefully lower the skewers, a few at a time, into the oil and fry the beef and peppers until they are crisp and golden brown. Remove from the oil and drain on kitchen towels.

Serve at once, piping hot.
Serves 4
Preparation and cooking time: 1½ hours

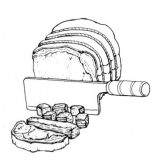

Bulgalbi

(Marinated Beef Spareribs)   (Korea)

Metric/Imperial	American
1kg./2lb. beef spareribs, cut into 7½cm./3in. pieces	2lb. beef spareribs, cut into 3in. pieces
1 Tbs. peanut oil	1 Tbs. peanut oil
MARINADE	MARINADE
4 Tbs. soya sauce	4 Tbs. soy sauce

3 garlic cloves, crushed	3 garlic cloves, crushed
2 Tbs. sake or dry white wine	2 Tbs. sake or dry white wine
4 Tbs. water	4 Tbs. water
2 tsp. roasted sesame seeds, ground	2 tsp. roasted sesame seeds, ground
2 Tbs. sugar	2 Tbs. sugar
1 tsp. black pepper	1 tsp. black pepper
4 spring onions, chopped	4 scallions, chopped
1 onion, chopped	1 onion, chopped
1 large ripe pear, peeled and cored	1 large ripe pear, peeled and cored

First prepare the spareribs. Using a sharp knife, carefully open out the flesh to make three 'wings', then criss-cross all of the meat (and bone) with small, deep incisions, taking care not to cut through the meat entirely.

To make the marinade, combine all the ingredients, except the pear, in a large, shallow dish. Chop the pear roughly so that the flesh is crumbling, and stir into the marinade mixture. Add the ribs and set aside to marinate overnight at room temperature.

Preheat the grill (broiler) to moderately high.

Remove the beef from the marinade and transfer to the rack of the grill (broiler). Brush lightly with the oil. Grill (broil) the meat for 15 minutes, or until it is cooked through and golden brown.

Remove from the heat and serve at once.

Serves 4
Preparation and cooking time: 13 hours

Oyi Jim

(Beef with Cucumbers)   (Korea)

Metric/Imperial	American
50ml./2fl.oz. vegetable oil	¼ cup vegetable oil
350g./12oz. rump steak, cut into thin strips	12oz. rump steak, cut into thin strips
2 medium cucumbers, halved lengthways with the seeds removed, then cut into 1cm./½in. slices	2 medium cucumbers, halved lengthways with the seeds removed, then cut into ½in. slices
1 red chilli, finely chopped	1 red chilli, finely chopped
1 Tbs. roasted sesame seeds, ground	1 Tbs. roasted sesame seeds, ground
MARINADE	MARINADE
1 Tbs. sesame oil	1 Tbs. sesame oil
1 Tbs. soya sauce	1 Tbs soy sauce
1 garlic clove, crushed	1 garlic clove, crushed
½ tsp. sugar	½ tsp. sugar

First, prepare the marinade. Combine all the ingredients together, beating until they are thoroughly blended. Arrange the beef strips in the marinade and baste and turn until they are covered. Set aside at room temperature for 15 minutes, turning the strips from time to time.

Heat the oil in a large frying-pan. When it is hot, add the beef mixture and stir-fry for 1½ minutes. Add the cucumbers and chilli and stir-fry for a further 2 minutes, or until the cucmbers are cooked but still crisp.

Transfer the mixture to a warmed serving dish and sprinkle over the ground sesame seeds before serving.

Serves 3–4
Preparation and cooking time: 35 minutes

Beef Teriyaki I

Metric/Imperial	American
1kg./2lb. fillet steak, cut into ½cm./¼in. slices	2lb. fillet steak, cut into ¼in. slices
MARINADE	MARINADE
2½cm./1in. piece of fresh root ginger, peeled and chopped	1in. piece of fresh green ginger, peeled and chopped
2 garlic cloves, crushed	2 garlic cloves, crushed
4 spring onions, finely chopped	4 scallions, finely chopped
25g./1oz. soft brown sugar	2 Tbs. soft brown sugar
250ml./8fl.oz. soya sauce	1 cup soy sauce
125ml./4fl.oz. sake or dry sherry	½ cup sake or dry sherry
salt and pepper	salt and pepper

Combine all the marinade ingredients in a large shallow dish. Put the steak pieces into the marinade and set aside at room temperature to marinate for 2 hours, basting occasionally.

Preheat the grill (broiler) to high.

Remove the steaks from the marinade and arrange them on the rack of the grill (broiler). Brush them generously with the marinade mixture and grill (broil) for 2 minutes. Remove from the heat, turn the steak and brush with the marinade. Grill (broil) for a further 2 minutes. These will give you rare steaks; double the cooking time for medium.

Transfer the steaks to warmed serving dishes and either serve at once, or cut into thin strips before serving.

Serves 6
Preparation and cooking time: 2¼ hours

Beef Teriyaki II

Metric/Imperial	American
4 small fillet steaks, cut ½cm./¼in. thick	4 small fillet steaks, cut ¼in. thick
3 Tbs. vegetable oil	3 Tbs. vegetable oil
MARINADE	MARINADE
50ml./2fl.oz. sake or dry sherry	¼ cup sake or dry sherry
2 Tbs. soya sauce	2 Tbs. soy sauce
1 garlic clove, crushed	1 garlic clove, crushed
50ml./2fl.oz. dashi	¼ cup dashi

Combine all the marinade ingredients in a large, shallow dish. Arrange the steaks in the mixture and set aside at room temperature to marinate for 1 hour, basting occasionally. Remove the steaks from the marinade, drying on kitchen towels, and reserve the marinade.

Heat the oil in a large frying-pan. When it is hot, add the steaks and fry for 1 minute on each side. Pour off all but a thin film of fat from the pan and add the marinade. Cook the steaks for a further 3 minutes on each side, basting them occasionally with the pan juices. These times will give rare steaks; double the cooking time for medium.

Transfer the steaks to warmed individual serving plates and either serve as they are or cut them into thin strips. Pour a little of the pan juices over the meat before serving.

Serves 4
Preparation and cooking time: 1¼ hours

Juhn Kol

(Mixed Meats and Vegetables cooked at the Table)   (Korea)

This popular dish has Japanese origins still represented today since the hibachi-type grill (broiler) plate on the table is a favourite way to present it. This is also a particularly suitable dish for barbecuing. The meats and vegetables suggested below are typical but any can be omitted or added to – the choice is yours.

Serve this superb Beef Teriyaki I with rice and bean sprouts for a delicious Japanese meal. If you wish to use chopsticks, you should cut the beef into thin strips before eating, as the Japanese do.

Metric/Imperial	American
½kg./1lb. rump steak or pork fillet (or a mixture of the two), cut into thin squares	1lb. rump steak or pork tenderloin (or a mixture of the two), cut into thin squares
2 large onions, sliced	2 large onions, sliced
3 celery stalks, cut into 2½cm./1in. lengths	3 celery stalks, cut into 1in. lengths
125g./4oz. small button mushrooms	1 cup small button mushrooms
2 carrots, thinly sliced diagonally	2 carrots, thinly sliced diagonally
MARINADE	MARINADE
125ml./4fl.oz. soya sauce	½ cup soy sauce
50g./2oz. sugar	¼ cup sugar
2 Tbs. vegetable oil	2 Tbs. vegetable oil
2 garlic cloves, crushed	2 garlic cloves, crushed
1 spring onion, finely chopped	1 scallion, finely chopped
1 chilli, finely chopped	1 chilli, finely chopped
1 Tbs. roasted sesame seeds, ground	1 Tbs. roasted sesame seeds, ground

First, prepare the marinade. Put all the marinade ingredients into a shallow mixing bowl and beat well until they are thoroughly blended. Add the meat squares to the mixture and baste well to cover them completely. Set aside for 2 hours, turning the squares from time to time.

Meanwhile, arrange all the vegetables attractively on a large platter and set on the table. Put the burner or electric plate on the table and warm up.

The meal is now ready to be cooked, ingredients requiring most cooking to be cooked first. The meat is first seared then cooked with enough of its marinade to keep from burning.

Serve hot.

Serves 4

Preparation and cooking time: 2½ hours

Binatok

(Dried Green Pea Pancake with Filling) (Korea)

Metric/Imperial	American
450g./1lb. dried split peas	2⅔ cups dried split peas
175g./6oz. long-grain rice	1 cup long-grain rice
2 garlic cloves, crushed	2 garlic cloves, crushed
2 spring onions, finely chopped	2 scallions, finely chopped
1 small onion, finely chopped	1 small onion, finely chopped
1 carrot, grated	1 carrot, grated
Water	Water
4 Tbs. peanut oil	4 Tbs. peanut oil
FILLING	FILLING
125g./4oz. rump steak, cut into thin strips	4oz. rump steak, cut into thin strips
3 spring onions, cut into 2½cm./1in. lengths	3 scallions, cut into 1 in. lengths
2 carrots, thinly sliced on the diagonal	2 carrots, thinly sliced on the diagonal
1 red or green pepper, pith and seeds removed and cut into strips	1 red or green pepper, pith and seeds removed and cut into strips
1 dried red chilli, crumbled	1 dried red chilli, crumbled
black pepper	black pepper
DIPPING SAUCE	DIPPING SAUCE
250 ml./8fl.oz. soya sauce	1 cup soy sauce
2 spring onions, very finely chopped	2 scallions, very finely chopped

Put the split peas and rice into a large bowl and just cover with water. Set aside to soak overnight. Drain, then put the mixture into a blender. Grind until smooth. Transfer the mixture to a large bowl. Stir in the garlic, spring onions (scallions), onion and carrot until they are well blended, then stir in enough water to form a thick batter. Set aside to 'rest' at room temperature for 30 minutes.

Meanwhile, assemble the filling ingredients on a large plate, in the order of cooking, that is those to be cooked longest first.

Heat quarter of the oil in a small saucepan. When it is very hot, add about a quarter of the batter and fry until the edges curl slightly. Arrange about a quarter of the meat over the batter and cook for 1 minute. Arrange a quarter of the spring onions (scallions), carrots, pepper and chilli, with pepper to taste, in the same way. Cook for 3 minutes, carefully working around the edges occasionally with a spatula, or until the bottom is brown. Carefully turn the pancake over and fry on the other side until it is golden brown.

Slide the pancake on to a warmed serving plate and keep hot while you cook the remaining batter and the remaining filling ingredients in the same way.

To make the dipping sauce, combine the soy sauce and spring onions (scallions) and pour into small, individual dipping bowls. Serve at once, with the bintatok.
Serves 4
Preparation and cooking time: 12¾ hours

Kan Juhn

(Fried Liver)   (Korea)

Metric/Imperial	American
½kg./1lb. lamb's liver, thinly sliced	1lb. lamb's liver, thinly sliced
1 large garlic clove	1 large garlic clove
salt and pepper	salt and pepper
50g./2oz. flour	½ cup flour
2 eggs, lightly beaten	2 eggs, lightly beaten
50ml./2fl.oz. sesame oil	¼ cup sesame oil
SAUCE	SAUCE
125ml./4fl.oz. soya sauce	½ cup soy sauce
125ml./4fl.oz. wine vinegar	½ cup wine vinegar
1 Tbs. soft brown sugar	1 Tbs. soft brown sugar
2 tsp. chopped pine nuts	2 tsp. chopped pine nuts

Rub the liver gently with the garlic, then discard the clove. Sprinkle with salt and pepper to taste. Dip the slices in flour, shaking off any excess, then in the beaten eggs.

Heat the oil in a large frying-pan. When it is hot, add the liver slices and fry for 3 to 4 minutes on each side (depending on thickness), or until the meat is just cooked through.

Meanwhile, make the sauce by combining all the ingredients in a screw-top jar until they are thoroughly blended. Pour into a shallow dipping bowl.

Transfer the liver slices to a warmed serving platter and serve at once, with the dipping sauce.
Serves 4
Preparation and cooking time: 20 minutes

Buta no Kakuni

(Pork Cooked with Sake)

Metric/Imperial	American
575g./1¼lb. lean pork meat, cut into 4 pieces	1¼lb. lean pork meat, cut into 4 pieces
4cm./1½in. piece of fresh root ginger, peeled and sliced	1½in. piece of fresh green ginger, peeled and sliced
2 garlic cloves, sliced	2 garlic cloves, sliced
450ml./15fl.oz. sake or dry sherry	2 cups sake or dry sherry
4 Tbs. sugar	4 Tbs. sugar
5 Tbs. soya sauce	5 Tbs. soy sauce
½ tsp. salt	½ tsp. salt
1 Tbs. mustard	1 Tbs. mustard

Put the pork into a medium saucepan and just cover with water. Add the ginger and garlic. Bring to the boil, reduce the heat to low and simmer for 1 hour. Remove from the heat, cool, then skim any fat from the surface of the liquid. Add the sake or sherry and sugar and continue to simmer for about 1½ hours, or until the meat is so tender that it is almost coming apart. Stir in the soy sauce and salt and remove the pan from the heat.

To serve, put one piece of pork on four individual, deep serving plates and pour over the cooking liquid. Add a dash of mustard to each piece of meat and serve at once.

Serves 4
Preparation and cooking time: 3½ hours

Ton-Yuk-Kui is a Korean dish of lean pork fillet (tenderloin), first marinated then baked until it is tender. It is tradionally served with a sauce made from the delicious marinade.

Ton-Yuk-Kui

(Korean Pork Fillets)

Metric/Imperial	American
1kg./2lb. pork fillet, thinly sliced	2lb. pork tenderloin, thinly sliced
2 Tbs. sesame oil	2 Tbs. sesame oil
MARINADE	MARINADE
125ml./4fl.oz. soya sauce	½ cup soy sauce
50 ml./2fl.oz. water	¼ cup water
3 Tbs. sugar	3 Tbs. sugar
2 spring onions, finely chopped	2 scallions, finely chopped
2 garlic cloves, crushed	2 garlic cloves, crushed
5cm./2in. piece of fresh root ginger, peeled and finely chopped	2in. piece of fresh green ginger, peeled and finely chopped
salt and pepper	salt and pepper

Combine all the marinade ingredients in a shallow dish and add the pork slices. Baste well, then set aside at room temperature for 2 hours, basting occasionally.

Preheat the oven to fairly hot 190°C (Gas Mark 5, 375°F).

Remove the pork from the marinade and dry on kitchen towels. Reserve the marinade.

Coat the bottom and sides of a baking dish with the oil. Arrange the pork slices in the dish, in one layer. Cover and bake the meat for 45 minutes to 1 hour, or until it is tender.

Meanwhile, pour the marinade into a saucepan and bring to the boil. Reduce the heat to low and simmer for 10 to 15 minutes, or until it has reduced slightly.

Remove the meat from the oven and arrange it on a warmed serving dish. Pour the cooking juices into the saucepan with the marinade and bring to the boil again. Pour a little over the pork and serve the rest with the meat.

Serves 4–6

Preparation and cooking time: 3¼ hours

Tonkatsu

(Japanese Pork Schnitzel)

The schnitzels are divided into thin strips before serving in the recipe below to enable chop-stick users to pick up the meat easily. If you plan to eat your meal with a knife and fork, this step can be omitted.

Metric/Imperial	American
6 large slices of pork fillet, beaten thin	6 large slices of pork tenderloin, beaten thin
2 eggs, beaten	2 eggs, beaten
2 Tbs. finely chopped spring onion	2 Tbs. finely chopped scallion
125g./4oz. soft white breadcrumbs	2 cups soft white breadcrumbs
75ml./3fl.oz. vegetable oil	⅓ cup vegetable oil
hichimi togarishi or paprika (to garnish)	hichimi togarishi or paprika (to garnish)
MARINADE	MARINADE
6 Tbs. soya sauce	6 Tbs. soy sauce
4 Tbs. mirin or sweet sherry	4 Tbs. mirin or sweet sherry
2 garlic cloves, crushed	2 garlic cloves, crushed
1 tsp. hichimi togarishi or paprika	1 tsp. hichimi togarishi or paprika

To make the marinade, combine the soy sauce, mirin or sherry, garlic and hichimi togarishi or paprika together, beating until they are thoroughly blended. Arrange the pork slices in the marinade and set aside at room temperature for 20 minutes, basting and turning the pork occasionally. Remove from the marinade and pat dry with kitchen towels. Discard the marinade.

Beat the eggs and spring onion (scallion) together in a shallow bowl. Dip the pork, first in the egg then in the breadcrumbs, shaking off any excess. Arrange the coated pork pieces on a plate and chill in the refrigerator for 2 hours.

Heat the oil in a large frying-pan. When it is hot, add the schnitzels and fry for 3 to 4 minutes on each side, or until they are golden brown and crisp. Remove from the heat and drain on kitchen towels.

Cut the schnitzels, crosswise, into thin strips, then carefully reassemble into the schnitzel shape. Serve at once, garnished with hichimi togarishi to taste.

Serves 4

Preparation and cooking time: 2½ hours

Kulbi Jim

(Spareribs with Sesame Seed Sauce)   (Korea)

This is a very basic version of a very popular dish. If you wish, vegetables can be added to the mixture – some sliced carrots or mushrooms, for instance, or even water chestnuts.

Metric/Imperial	American
3 Tbs. vegetable oil	3 Tbs. vegetable oil
1½kg./3lb. American-style spareribs, cut into 5cm./2in. pieces	3lb. spareribs, cut into 2-rib serving pieces
2 Tbs. sugar	2 Tbs. sugar
2 Tbs. sesame oil	2 Tbs. sesame oil
4 Tbs. soya sauce	4 Tbs. soy sauce
3 spring onions, chopped	3 scallions, chopped
2 garlic cloves, crushed	2 garlic cloves, crushed
2½cm./1in. piece of fresh root ginger, peeled and chopped	1in. piece of fresh green ginger, peeled and chopped
3 Tbs. roasted sesame seeds, ground	3 Tbs. roasted sesame seeds, ground
300ml./10fl.oz. water	1¼ cups water

Heat the oil in a large, shallow saucepan or frying-pan. When it is hot, add the spareribs and fry until they are evenly browned. (If necessary, fry the ribs in two or three batches.)

Stir in the sugar, sesame oil, soy sauce, spring onions (scallions), garlic, ginger and 2 tablespoons of the sesame seeds until they are thoroughly blended. Pour over the water and bring to the boil. Reduce the heat to low, cover the pan and simmer the mixture for 50 minutes, or until the spareribs are cooked and crisp.

Transfer the mixture to a warmed serving dish and sprinkle over the remaining roasted sesame seeds before serving.
Serves 6–8
Preparation and cooking time: 1½ hours

Seekumche Kuk

(Spinach with Pork)   (Korea)

Many Korean dishes, like most Chinese ones, are geared to make comparatively little meat go quite a long way – and this dish is a particularly good example. If you prefer, lean beef, such as rump steak, can be substituted for the pork.

Metric/Imperial	American
1kg./2lb. spinach, washed thoroughly and chopped	2lb. spinach, washed thoroughly and chopped
1 tsp. salt	1 tsp. salt
3 Tbs. vegetable oil	3 Tbs. vegetable oil
225g./8oz. pork fillet, cut into bite-sized pieces	8oz. pork tenderloin, cut into bite-sized pieces
1 garlic clove, crushed	1 garlic clove, crushed
¼ tsp. cayenne pepper	¼ tsp. cayenne pepper
2 spring onions, chopped	2 scallions, chopped
2 Tbs. soya sauce	2 Tbs. soy sauce
½ tsp. sugar	½ tsp. sugar
2 Tbs. roasted sesame seeds, ground	2 Tbs. roasted sesame seeds, ground

Put the spinach into a large saucepan with the salt and cook gently for 8 to 10 minutes, or until it is just tender. (Do not add water – there should be enough clinging to the leaves to provide moisture for cooking.) Drain, then transfer the spinach to a plate. Keep hot.

Heat the oil in a large frying-pan. When it is hot, add the pork pieces and garlic and stir-fry for 2 minutes. Stir in the cayenne, spring onions (scallions), soy sauce and sugar and continue to stir-fry for a further 2 minutes. Stir in the chopped spinach and heat it through.

Transfer the mixture to a warmed serving dish and sprinkle over the roasted sesame seeds before serving.

Serves 3–4
Preparation and cooking time: 25 minutes

Yakibuta

(Basted Pork)

Metric/Imperial	American
1kg./2lb. boned leg or loin of pork	2lb. boned leg or loin of pork
3 garlic cloves, crushed	3 garlic cloves, crushed
4cm./1½in. piece of fresh root ginger, peeled and sliced	1½in. piece of fresh green ginger, peeled and sliced
150ml./5fl.oz. sake or dry sherry	⅔ cup sake or dry sherry
150ml./5fl.oz. soya sauce	⅔ cup soy sauce
2 Tbs. sugar	2 Tbs. sugar
1½ tsp. salt	1½ tsp. salt

Put the pork piece in a large saucepan and just cover with water. Add the garlic and ginger. Bring to the boil, then cook over moderate heat for 1 hour, or until the water has evaporated and the oil on the bottom of the saucepan begins to bubble. Pour off the oil and turn the meat in the pan, slightly burning the outside.

Warm the sake or sherry to tepid then add to the saucepan. Continue cooking until the sake has boiled away. Turn the meat again, basting with the pan juices. Stir in the remaining ingredients and cook for a further 10 minutes.

Serve either hot or cold.

Serves 6–8
Preparation and cooking time: 1¾ hours

Goma Yaki

(Chicken with Sesame Seeds)

Metric/Imperial	American
2 large chicken breasts, skinned, boned and halved	2 large chicken breasts, skinned boned and halved
3 Tbs. sesame oil	3 Tbs. sesame oil
2 Tbs. roasted sesame seeds	2 Tbs. roasted sesame seeds
MARINADE	MARINADE
75ml./3fl.oz. sake or dry sherry	⅓ cup sake or dry sherry
2 tsp. soya sauce	2 tsp. soy sauce
monosodium glutamate (optional)	MSG (optional)
¼ tsp. hichimi togarishi or paprika	¼ tsp. hichimi togarishi or paprika

First, prepare the marinade. Combine all the ingredients in a medium-sized shallow bowl, beating until they are thoroughly blended. Add the chicken pieces and baste well. Set aside at room temperature for 20 minutes, turning and basting the chicken from time to time.

Heat the oil in a large frying-pan. When it is hot, add the chicken pieces and fry for 5 minutes on each side. Sprinkle over half the sesame seeds and stir and turn until the chicken is coated. Reduce the heat to low and cook the chicken for a further 6 to 8 minutes, or until the pieces are cooked through and tender.

Transfer the mixture to a warmed serving dish and sprinkle over the remaining sesame seeds before serving.

Serves 2-4
Preparation and cooking time: 50 minutes

Dak Jim

(Steamed Chicken and Vegetables)   (Korea)

Metric/Imperial	American
1 x 2kg./4lb. chicken, cut into 8 or 10 serving pieces	1 x 4lb. chicken, cut into 8 or 10 serving pieces
2 carrots, cut into thin strips	2 carrots, cut into thin strips
3 dried mushrooms, soaked in cold water for 30 minutes, drained and thinly sliced	3 dried mushrooms, soaked in cold water for 30 minutes, drained and thinly sliced
1 bamboo shoot, sliced	1 bamboo shoot, sliced
2 spring onions, thinly sliced	2 scallions, thinly sliced
2 garlic cloves, crushed	2 garlic cloves, crushed
1 tsp. ground ginger	1 tsp. ground ginger
50g./2oz. walnuts, chopped	⅓ cup chopped walnuts
50ml./2fl. oz. soya sauce	¼ cup soy sauce
2 Tbs. soft brown sugar	2 Tbs. soft brown sugar
1 Tbs. roasted sesame seeds, ground	1 Tbs. roasted sesame seeds, ground
salt and pepper	salt and pepper
GARNISH	GARNISH
2 eggs, separated	2 eggs, separated

Put the chicken pieces into a saucepan and cover with water. Bring to the boil, cover and simmer for 1 to 1½ hours, or until the chicken is tender. Drain and reserve the stock. When the meat is cool enough to handle, cut the chicken into bite-sized strips.

Put all the remaining ingredients, except the garnish, into a large saucepan and bring to the boil. Stir in the chicken strips and reserved stock, cover and simmer for 15 to 20 minutes or until the vegetables are cooked but still crisp.

Meanwhile, make the garnish. Beat the egg yolks and whites separately until they are both well mixed. Lightly oil a heavy-bottomed frying-pan and heat it over moderate heat. Pour in the egg white and spread over the bottom in a thin layer. Cook until the bottom is firm, then turn over and cook until the other side is firm. Slide on to a warmed dish and cook the egg yolks in the same way. Cut the cooked eggs into strips.

Transfer the chicken and vegetables to a warmed serving bowl and scatter over the egg strips before serving.

Serves 6
Preparation and cooking time: 2½ hours

Chicken Teriyaki I

Metric/Imperial	American
125ml./4fl.oz. sake or dry sherry	½ cup sake or dry sherry
50ml./2fl.oz. soya sauce	¼ cup soy sauce
125ml./4fl.oz. dashi	½ cup dashi
2 tsp. sugar	2 tsp. sugar
2 tsp. cornflour	2 tsp. cornstarch
4 chicken breasts, skinned and boned	4 chicken breasts, skinned and boned
2 celery stalks, sliced lengthways	2 celery stalks, sliced lengthways
8 spring onions, trimmed	8 scallions, trimmed

The essence of Japanese cooking is well illustrated in this dish of Chicken Teriyaki I – the simpliclty of the presentation and the importance attached to the appearance of the dish. If you wish to eat with chopsticks, cut the meat (to the bone) into thin strips.

Warm the sake or sherry in a small saucepan. Remove from the heat and carefully ignite, allowing the sake to burn until the flames die down. Stir in the soy sauce and dashi. Put 3 tablespoons of the sake mixture into a small bowl and mix in the sugar and cornflour (cornstarch). Set aside. Pour the remaining sauce into a shallow dish.

Preheat the grill (broiler) to moderately high.

Dip the chicken pieces into the sauce to coat thoroughly, then arrange them on the rack in the grill (broiler). Grill (broil) for about 6 minutes, or until one side is golden brown. Remove the chicken from the heat, coat thoroughly in the sauce again and return to the rack. Grill (broil) the other side for 6 minutes, or until it is golden brown. Remove from the heat again and dip into the sauce then return to the grill (broiler). Brush generously with the cornflour (cornstarch) mixture and grill (broil) for a final 6 minutes, turning the chicken occasionally, or until the meat is cooked through.

Arrange the chicken pieces on a warmed serving plate and either serve as is, or cut into slices. Garnish with the celery and spring onions (scallions).
Serves 4
Preparation and cooking time : 45 minutes

Chicken Teriyaki II

Metric/Imperial	American
2 Tbs. clear honey	2 Tbs. clear honey
6 small chicken breasts, skinned and boned	6 small chicken breasts, skinned and boned
MARINADE	MARINADE
125ml./4fl. oz. soya sauce	½ cup soy sauce
salt and pepper	salt and pepper
4cm./1½in. piece of fresh root ginger, peeled and chopped	1½in. piece of fresh green ginger, peeled and chopped
1 garlic clove, crushed	1 garlic clove, crushed
125ml./4fl. oz. sake or dry white wine	½ cup sake or dry white wine

Combine all the marinade ingredients in a large shallow dish and set aside.

Heat the honey in a small saucepan until it liquefies slightly. Remove the pan from the heat and brush the honey mixture generously over the chicken breasts. Arrange the chicken in the marinade and set aside at room temperature to marinate for 2 hours, basting occasionally.

Preheat the oven to moderate 180°C (Gas Mark 4, 350°F).

Line a deep-sided baking pan with foil and arrange the chicken breasts on the foil. Pour over the marinade. Put the pan into the oven and bake, basting frequently, for 30 to 35 minutes, or until the chicken is cooked through and tender. Remove from the oven and, using a slotted spoon, transfer the chicken to a warmed serving dish. Pour the cooking juices into a warmed serving bowl and serve with the chicken.

Serves 6
Preparation and cooking time: 2¾ hours

Chicken Pokkum

(Stir-Fried Chicken)   (Korea)

Metric/Imperial	American
50ml./2fl.oz. sesame oil	¼ cup sesame oil
2 chicken breasts, skinned, boned and cut into strips	2 chicken breasts, skinned, boned and cut into strips
2 spring onions, chopped	2 scallions, chopped
1 garlic clove, crushed	1 garlic clove, crushed
4cm./1½in. piece of fresh root ginger, peeled and finely chopped	1½in. piece of fresh green ginger, peeled and finely chopped
50g./2oz. button mushrooms, sliced	½ cup sliced button mushrooms
3 Tbs. soya sauce	3 Tbs. soy sauce
2 Tbs. water	2 Tbs. water
1 Tbs. sugar	1 Tbs. sugar
1 Tbs. roasted sesame seeds, ground	1 Tbs. roasted sesame seeds, ground

Heat the oil in a large frying-pan. When it is hot, add the chicken strips and stir-fry for 3 minutes, or until they are just cooked through. Stir in the spring onions (scallions), garlic and ginger and stir-fry for 1 minute. Add the mushrooms and stir-fry for 2 minutes. Stir in the soy sauce, water, sugar and sesame seeds and bring to the boil. Cook for 1 minute.

Transfer the mixture to a warmed serving dish and serve at once.

Serves 3–4
Preparation and cooking time: 15 minutes

Yaki Tori

(Barbecued Chicken)

Metric/Imperial	American
½kg./1lb. chicken breast, skinned, boned and cut into bite-sized pieces	1lb. chicken breast , skinned, boned and cut into bite-sized pieces
½kg./1lb. leeks, cleaned, cut into 1cm./½in. lengths and parboiled	1lb. leeks, cleaned, cut into ½in. lengths and parboiled
SAUCE	SAUCE
175ml./6fl. oz. soya sauce	¾ cup soy sauce
175ml./6fl. oz. mirin or sweet sherry	¾ cup mirin or sweet sherry
monosodium glutamate (optional)	MSG (optional)

Thread the chicken pieces on to small skewers. Thread the leek pieces (pierce through the sides) on to separate small skewers. Set aside.

Preheat the grill (broiler) to moderately high.

Meanwhile, to make the sauce, put the soy sauce and mirin into a small saucepan and add monosodium glutamate to taste. Bring to the boil, then cook for a few minutes or until it begins to thicken slightly. Remove from the heat.

Arrange the chicken and leek skewers on the rack of the grill (broiler). (If possible put the leeks further away from the flame to avoid excessive charring.) Grill (broil) for 3 minutes. Remove the skewers from the heat and dip into the sauce mixture, to coat the food thoroughly. Return to the heat, turn the skewers and grill (broil) for a further 3 minutes. Repeat this once more, then cook until the chicken meat is cooked through.

Remove from the heat and dip the skewers once more in the sauce mixture before serving.

Serves 4
Preparation and cooking time: 40 minutes
Note: Lamb or calf's liver and green pepper pieces can also be cooked in this way.

Iri Dori

(Chicken Casserole)

Any vegetables can be used in this dish – variations could include onions, cauliflower and brussels sprouts.

Metric/Imperial	American
50ml./2fl.oz. vegetable oil	¼ cup vegetable oil
2 small chicken breasts, skinned, boned and cut into bite-sized pieces	2 small chicken breasts, skinned, boned and cut into bite-sized pieces
4 dried mushrooms, soaked in cold water for 30 minutes, drained, stalks removed and caps quartered	4 dried mushrooms, soaked in cold water for 30 minutes, drained, stalks removed and caps quartered
2 large carrots, diced	2 large carrots, diced
175g./6oz. tin bamboo shoot, drained and chopped	6oz. can bamboo shoot, drained and chopped
175ml./6fl.oz. dashi	¾ cup dashi
4 Tbs. mirin or sweet sherry	4 Tbs. mirin or sweet sherry
4 Tbs. sugar	4 Tbs. sugar
4 Tbs. soya sauce	4 Tbs. soy sauce
3 Tbs. green peas	3 Tbs. green peas

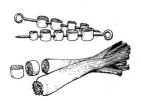

Heat the oil in a large, deep frying-pan. When it is hot, add the chicken pieces, mushrooms, carrots and bamboo shoot and fry, stirring occasionally, for 2 minutes. Add the dashi, mirin or sherry and sugar and cook for a further 10 minutes, stirring occasionally. Reduce the heat to low and stir in the soy sauce. Simmer the mixture until about three-quarters of the liquid has evaporated. Stir in the peas, then remove the pan from the heat.

Transfer the mixture to a warmed serving dish and serve at once.

Serves 4
Preparation and cooking time: 1 hour

Chicken Stew

(Korea)

Metric/Imperial	American
1 x 2kg./4lb. chicken, cut into 8 serving pieces	1 x 4lb. chicken, cut into 8 serving pieces
MARINADE	MARINADE
4 Tbs. soya sauce	4 Tbs. soy sauce
125ml./4fl.oz. water	½ cup water
½ small onion, chopped	½ small onion, chopped
2 spring onions, chopped	2 scallions, chopped
1 carrot, chopped	1 carrot, chopped
1 Tbs. sugar	1 Tbs. sugar
salt and pepper	salt and pepper
5cm./2in. piece of fresh root ginger, peeled and chopped	2in. piece of fresh green ginger, peeled and chopped
2 garlic cloves, crushed	2 garlic cloves, crushed

Put all the marinade ingredients into a saucepan and bring to the boil. Reduce the heat to moderately low and add the chicken pieces, basting thoroughly. Cover the pan and cook the mixture for 30 minutes. Remove from the heat and set aside to cool to room temperature. When the mixture is cool, chill in the refrigerator overnight.

Remove from the refrigerator and set over high heat. Bring to the boil. Reduce the heat to low and simmer the mixture for 20 to 30 minutes, or until the chicken is cooked through and tender.

Serve at once.

Serves 8
Preparation and cooking time: 13 hours

Tori no Sakamushi

(Sake-Steamed Chicken)

Metric/Imperial	American
4 chicken breasts, skinned, boned and cut into 2½cm./1in. slices	4 chicken breasts, skinned, boned and cut into 1in. slices
175ml./6fl.oz. sake or dry sherry	¾ cup sake or dry sherry
1 Tbs. sugar	1 Tbs. sugar
1 tsp. soya sauce	1 tsp. soy sauce
¼ tsp. monosodium glutamate (optional)	¼ tsp. MSG (optional)

Put the chicken meat slices into a shallow dish and pour over the sake or sherry. Set aside to marinate at room temperature for 1 hour, basting occasionally. Remove the chicken from the marinade and reserve the marinade. Pat the chicken dry with kitchen towels.

Arrange the chicken slices, in one layer, in the top part of a steamer, or on an ovenproof plate. Fill the base of the steamer (or a medium saucepan over which the plate will fit) about two-thirds full of boiling water and fit the top part over. Cover and steam the meat for 10 minutes. Remove the steamer from the heat and set aside.

Preheat the grill (broiler) to high.

Pour the reserved marinade into a small saucepan and stir in the sugar, soy sauce and monosodium glutamate. Bring to the boil, stirring constantly, then remove from the heat.

Arrange the chicken slices on the rack of the grill (broiler), brush with the marinade sauce and grill (broil) for 3 minutes on each side, basting occasionally with the sauce.

To serve, transfer the chicken slices to a warmed serving dish and pour over the remaining sauce.
Serves 4
Preparation and cooking time: 1½ hours.

Tori No Sakamushi (Sake-Steamed Chicken) is first steamed then barbecued to crisp perfection. Serve as either a first course or hors d'oeuvre in the West, or as part of an Oriental meal.

FISH

Shimesaba

(Marinated Mackerel)

Metric/Imperial	American
1 large fresh mackerel, cleaned, gutted and filleted	1 large fresh mackerel, cleaned, gutted and filleted
1 tsp. salt	1 tsp. salt
450ml./15fl.oz. white wine vinegar	2 cups white wine vinegar
4cm./1½in. piece of fresh root ginger, peeled and grated	1½in. piece of fresh green ginger, peeled and grated
4 spring onions, finely chopped	4 scallions, finely chopped
250ml./8fl.oz. soya sauce	1 cup soy sauce
2 tsp. green horseradish (wasabi), mixed to a paste with 2 tsp. water	2 tsp. green horseradish (wasabi), mixed to a paste with 2 tsp. water

Sprinkle the mackerel fillets liberally with salt and put into the refrigerator for 1 hour. Remove from the refrigerator and wash under cold running water. Arrange the fillets in a shallow dish and pour over the vinegar. Soak for 1 hour, turning at least once.

Remove the mackerel from the vinegar and pat dry on kitchen towels. Skin and remove any bones with your fingers. Cut across each fillet at about 2½cm./1in. intervals and arrange the pieces decoratively on a serving dish. Garnish with the grated ginger and spring onions (scallions).

Pour the soy sauce into individual dipping bowls and arrange the horseradish in individual small bowls. To make the dipping sauce, mix the horseradish and soy sauce together to taste and dip in the fish.

Serves 4
Preparation and cooking time: 2¼ hours

Hizakana

(Fish Simmered in Soy Sauce)

If you prefer, other fish such as mackerel, sole and sardine can be used instead of herrings in this dish.

Metric/Imperial	American
4 herrings, gutted and cleaned	4 herrings, gutted and cleaned
4cm./1½in. piece of fresh root ginger, peeled and sliced	1½in. piece of fresh green ginger, peeled and sliced
SAUCE	SAUCE
250ml./8fl.oz. dashi	1 cup dashi
250ml./8fl.oz. soya sauce	1 cup soy sauce
250ml./8fl.oz. sake or dry sherry	1 cup sake or dry sherry
3 tsp. sugar	3 tsp. sugar
monosodium glutamate (optional)	MAG (optional)

Put the fish on a chopping board and make two or three cuts through the belly of each one, to allow the sauce to be absorbed while cooking. Set aside.

Put the dashi, soy sauce, sake or sherry, sugar and monosodium glutamate to taste in a saucepan large enough to accommodate the fish. Bring to the boil. Arrange the fish in the bottom of the pan and sprinkle over the ginger slices. Return the dashi mixture to the boil, reduce the heat to low and simmer for 5 minutes. Reduce the heat to very low and continue to simmer for a further 15 minutes.

Transfer the fish to a warmed deep serving dish and pour over some of the cooking liquid. Serve at once.

Serves 4
Preparation and cooking time: 30 minutes

Sansuhn Jim

(Fish with Vegetables)   (Korea)

Metric/Imperial	American
225g./8oz. braising beef, cut into thin strips	8oz. chuck steak, cut into thin strips
125g./4oz. button mushrooms, sliced	1 cup sliced button mushrooms,
3 celery stalks, chopped	3 celery stalks, chopped
1 small turnip or large Japanese radish, chopped	1 small turnip or large Japanese radish, chopped
2 carrots, sliced	2 carrots, sliced
½kg./1lb. fish fillets, cut into small bite-sized pieces	1lb. fish fillets, cut into small bite-sized pieces
4 spring onions, chopped	4 scallions, chopped
2 green chillis, finely chopped	2 green chillis, finely chopped
3 Tbs. soya sauce	3 Tbs. soy sauce
MARINADE	MARINADE
2 tsp. sugar	2 tsp. sugar
2 Tbs. soya sauce	2 Tbs. soy sauce
1 garlic clove, crushed	1 garlic clove, crushed
2 Tbs. sesame oil	2 Tbs. sesame oil
1 Tbs. roasted sesame seeds, ground	1 Tbs. roasted sesame seeds, ground

First, prepare the marinade. Combine all the ingredients in a shallow bowl, beating until they are thoroughly blended. Arrange the beef strips in the marinade, basting and turning to coat them. Set aside at room temperature for 20 minutes, basting and turning the strips from time to time.

Preheat the oven to moderate 180°C (Gas Mark 4, 350°F).

Arrange the beef mixture in the bottom of a medium-sized flameproof casserole. Cover with a layer of mushrooms, then celery, turnip or radish and sliced carrots. Arrange the fish pieces on top and scatter over about three-quarters of the spring onions (scallions) and chillis. Pour just enough water into the casserole to come about half-way up the mixture then add the soy sauce. Bring to the boil on top of the stove, then cover and put into the oven. Cook for 15 to 20 minutes, or until the fish flakes easily.

Remove from the oven and garnish with the remaining spring onions (scallions) and chillis before serving.

Serves 4–6
Preparation and cooking time: 1 hour

(See previous page) Yok
Kai Chi Sake (Marinated
Salmon) is raw, delicate
salmon marinated to the
succulence of rare beef in a
mixture of soy sauce
and sake.

Yok Kai Sake

(Marinated Salmon)

Metric/Imperial	American
½kg./1lb. fresh salmon, thinly sliced then cut into strips	1lb. fresh salmon, thinly sliced then cut into strips
2½cm./1in. piece of fresh root ginger, peeled and chopped	1in. piece of fresh green ginger, peeled and chopped
1 garlic clove, crushed	1 garlic clove, crushed
2 spring onions, chopped	2 scallions, chopped
1 tsp. sugar	1 tsp. sugar
1 tsp. salt	1 tsp. salt
50ml./2fl.oz. soya sauce	¼ cup soy sauce
150ml./5fl.oz. sake or dry sherry	⅔ cup sake or dry sherry

Arrange the salmon strips in a large shallow serving dish. Combine all of the remaining ingredients in a mixing bowl, beating until they are well blended and the sugar has dissolved. Pour the mixture over the salmon strips and put the dish into the refrigerator for 1 hour.

Remove from the refrigerator and serve at once.

Serves 4
Preparation time: 1¼ hours

Fish in Wine Sauce

Metric/Imperial	American
4 large herrings, cleaned, gutted and filleted	4 large herrings, cleaned, gutted and filleted
4 Tbs. sake or dry sherry	4 Tbs. sake or dry sherry
4 Tbs. mirin or sweet sherry	4 Tbs. mirin or sweet sherry
125ml./4fl.oz. soya sauce	½ cup soy sauce
2 Tbs. sugar	2 Tbs. sugar
1 tsp. black pepper	1 tsp. black pepper
1 Tbs. chopped parsley	1 Tbs. chopped parsley
1 tsp. chopped chives	1 tsp. chopped chives

Wipe the herrings with damp kitchen towels and place on a chopping board. Cut each one in two lengthways. Make three cuts on the skin side of each fish, taking care not to cut through the flesh completely. Set aside.

Put the sake or sherry and mirin or sherry into a small saucepan and bring to the boil. Remove from the heat and ignite carefully. Leave until the flames have died down, then stir in the soy sauce and sugar. Pour the mixture into a shallow mixing bowl.

Preheat the grill (broiler) to moderate.

Dip the herring into the sauce mixture, then arrange them on the rack of the grill (broiler). Grill (broil) for 5 minutes. Remove the fish from the heat and dip into the sauce again. Return to the heat, turn the fish and grill (broil) for a further 5 minutes.

Transfer the fish to a warmed serving dish and garnish with the pepper, parsley and chives. Pour the basting liquid into a warmed serving bowl and serve with the fish.

Serves 4
Preparation and cooking time: 40 minutes

Misozuke

(Barbecued Mackerel with Miso)

Although mackerel has been suggested as the fish in the recipe given below, any similar, rather oily fish could be substituted – herrings, fresh large sardines, or even red mullet. This dish can be served either as an hors d'oeuvre (in which case it will serve 8) or as a main course.

Metric/Imperial	American
4 mackerel, cleaned, gutted and cut into 5cm./2in. pieces	4 mackerel, cleaned, gutted and cut into 2in. pieces
MARINADE	MARINADE
125g./4oz. miso paste	½ cup miso paste
50g./2oz. sugar	¼ cup sugar
2 Tbs. sake or dry sherry	2 Tbs. sake or dry sherry
2 Tbs. mirin or sweet sherry	2 Tbs. mirin or sweet sherry

First, make the marinade. Combine all the ingredients in a large shallow mixing bowl, beating until they are thoroughly blended. Arrange the fish pieces in the marinade, basting to coat them completely. Cover the dish and chill in the refrigerator for at least one day, turning the fish pieces from time to time. Remove the fish pieces from the marinade and pat dry with kitchen towels. Discard the marinade.

Preheat the grill (broiler) to moderate. Arrange the fish pieces on the rack of the grill (broiler) and grill (broil) for 5 minutes. Turn the fish over and grill (broil) for a further 5 to 8 minutes, or until the fish flesh flakes easily.

Transfer the fish pieces to a warmed serving dish and serve at once.

Serves 4
Preparation and cooking time: 24½ hours

Sakana Shioyaki

(Fish Barbecued with Salt)

This is another very simple yet very popular way of preparing fish in Japan, and is very healthy since the natural flavour of the fish is preserved. The salt is also said to break down the fats under the skin of the fish, and thereby moisten the flesh.

Metric/Imperial	American
4 herrings, cleaned and gutted	4 herrings, cleaned and gutted
3 Tbs. salt	3 Tbs. salt

Wash the fish under cold running water, then pat dry with kitchen towels. Cover liberally with salt (use more than suggested if you wish) and set aside at room temperature for at least 30 minutes.

Preheat the grill (broiler) to moderate.

Wipe any excess liquid from the fish and sprinkle with a little more salt, rubbing it well into the tail to prevent burning. Grill (broil) the fish for 15 to 20 minutes, turning occasionally, or until the flesh flakes easily.

Serve at once, with rice, soup and some vegetable side dishes.

Serves 4
Preparation and cooking time: 50 minutes

Washi no Su-Jyoyu Zuke

(Barbecued Sardines)

Metric/Imperial	American
150ml./5fl.oz. soya sauce	$\frac{2}{3}$ cup soy sauce
50ml./2fl.oz. vinegar	$\frac{1}{4}$ cup vinegar
2 Tbs. lemon juice	2 Tbs. lemon juice
2½cm./1in. piece of fresh root ginger, peeled and chopped	1in. piece of fresh green ginger, peeled and chopped
2 garlic cloves, crushed	2 garlic cloves, crushed
½kg./1lb. fresh sardines, cleaned and gutted	1lb. fresh sardines, cleaned and gutted
2 Tbs. vegetable oil	2 Tbs. vegetable oil

Combine the soy sauce, vinegar, lemon juice, ginger and garlic in a small bowl. Arrange the sardines in a large shallow dish and pour over the soy sauce mixture, basting to coat the fish thoroughly. Set aside at room temperature to marinate for 2 hours, basting the fish occasionally.

Preheat the grill (broiler) to high.

Remove the sardines from the marinade and dry them on kichen towels. Discard the marinade. Reduce the grill (broiler) to moderate.

Arrange the sardines on the rack of the grill (broiler) and brush the fish with half the oil. Grill (broil) for 4 minutes, then brush again with the remaining oil. Grill (broil) the other side for 3 minutes, or until the flesh flakes easily.

Remove from the heat and serve at once.

Serves 4

Preparation and cooking time: $2\frac{1}{4}$ hours

Washi No Su-Jyoyu Zuke is a delicious dish of sardines marinated first in a mixture of soy sauce, vinegar, lemon juice and ginger, then barbecued.

64

Ika no Tsukeyaki

(Gilled [Broiled] Squid)

Metric/Imperial	American
4 medium squid, cleaned, spinal bone removed	4 medium squid, cleaned, spinal bone removed
4 Tbs. grated radish	4 Tbs. grated radish
MARINADE	MARINADE
150ml./5fl.oz. soya sauce	⅔ cup soy sauce
150ml./5fl.oz. sake or dry sherry	⅔ cup sake or dry sherry
2 Tbs. sugar	2 Tbs. sugar

Remove the tentacles from the squid, then rub away the outer skin. Set side.

Put the soy sauce, sake or sherry and sugar into a small saucepan and bring to the boil. Remove the pan from the heat and pour the mixture into a large shallow dish. Arrange the squid in the dish and set aside at room temperature to marinate for 15 minutes.

Preheat the grill (broiler) to moderate.

Remove the squid from the marinade and pat dry with kitchen towels. Reserve the marinade. Score the surface of the fish and arrange them on the rack of the grill (broiler). Grill (broil) for 8 minutes on each side, basting occasionally with the marinating liquid.

Remove the squid to a chopping board and cut into strips about 2½cm./1in. wide. Arrange decoratively on a serving platter and pour over the remaining marinade. Garnish with grated radish and serve at once.

Serves 4
Preparation and cooking time: 30 minutes

Tarako to Tasai no Niawase

(Cod's Roes and Vegetables Cooked in Soy Sauce)

Metric/Imperial	American
3 Tbs. vegetable oil	3 Tbs. vegetable oil
1 large carrot, cut into matchstick strips	1 large carrot, cut into matchstick strips
50g./2oz. tin shirataki noodles, soaked in hot water for 3 minutes and cut into matchstick strips	2oz. can shirataki noodles, soaked in hot water for 3 minutes and cut into matchstick strips
1 Tbs. sake or dry sherry	1 Tbs. sake or dry sherry
monosodium glutamate (optional)	MSG (optional)
2 fresh cod's roes, skinned	2 fresh cod's roes, skinned
250ml./8fl.oz. dashi	1 cup dashi
2 Tbs. soya sauce	2 Tbs. soy sauce
1 Tbs. mirin or sweet sherry	1 Tbs. mirin or sweet sherry
1 leek, cleaned and finely chopped	1 leek, cleaned and finely chopped

Heat the oil in a deep frying-pan. When it is hot, add the carrot, shirataki, sake or sherry and monosodium glutamate to taste. Cook, stirring occasionally, for 5 minutes. Add the cod's roes, dashi, soy sauce and mirin and continue to cook until the roes turn white. Stir in the leek and cook for a further 2 minutes.

Transfer the mixture to a warmed serving bowl and serve.

Serves 4-6
Preparation and cooking time: 30 minutes

Sashimi

(Sliced Raw Fish)

Sashimi is one of the finest and simplest of Japanese fish dishes. Almost any type of fish can be used – dover sole, lemon sole, tuna, squid, abalone, bream or any type of shellfish – but it must be of the very highest quality and be as fresh as possible. To preserve freshness, it is better to buy a whole fish and have the fish merchant clean and fillet it for you, rather than purchase pre-filleted fish.

Metric/Imperial	American
½kg./1lb. firm fresh fish (as above)	1lb. firm fresh fish (as above)
1 Tbs. salt	1 Tbs. salt
SAUCE	SAUCE
2 tsp. green horseradish (wasabi), mixed to a paste with 2 tsp. water	2 tsp. green horseradish (wasabi), mixed to a paste with 2 tsp. water
125ml./4fl.oz. soya sauce	½ cup soy sauce

Sashimi (Sliced Raw Fish) – the dish that foreigners (rightly) think of as epitomizing Japanese cuisine. Here the fish is as fresh from the sea as possible, and served with a slightly piquant sauce made from horseradish and soy sauce.

Wash the fillets and sprinkle them lightly with salt. Cover and put into the refrigerator for 30 minutes. (Some people prefer to douse the fish in boiling water, then refresh in cold running water before putting into the refrigerator, to provide protection against surface bacteria.)

Remove the fish from the refrigerator and cut crosswise into bite-sized pieces. Arrange the pieces either on one large serving dish or on individual dishes.

To make the sauce, mix the horseradish into the soy sauce, then pour the mixture into individual dipping bowls. The fish should be dipped in the sauce before eating.

Serves 2-4

Preparation time: 40 minutes

Sushi

(Marinated Fish)

Metric/Imperial	American
½kg./1lb. mackerel fillets, skinned	1lb. mackerel fillets, skinned
GARNISH	GARNISH
125g./4oz. radish, grated	⅔ cup grated radish
1 red pepper, pith and seeds removed and chopped	1 red pepper, pith and seeds removed and chopped
2 Tbs. soya sauce mixed with 2 tsp. lemon juice	2 Tbs. soy sauce mixed with 2 tsp. lemon juice
SAUCE	SAUCE
2 tsp. green horseradish (wasabi), mixed to a paste with 2 tsp. water	2 tsp. green horseradish (washabi), mixed to a paste with 2 tsp. water
50ml./2fl.oz. soya sauce mixed with 2 Tbs. sake or dry sherry	¼ cup soy sauce mixed with 2 Tbs. sake or dry sherry

Put the mackerel fillets in a colander and pour over boiling water. Refresh the fish under cold running-water, then transfer them to a chopping board. Cut the fillets, crosswise, into very thin strips. Arrange the strips on a plate, cover with foil and chill in the refrigerator while you arrange the garnish.

Put the vegetables in a small serving bowl and pour over the soy sauce mixture. Toss gently so that all the vegetable pieces are coated.

Remove the fish from the refrigerator and divide it among six individual serving bowls. Arrange a portion of the garnish beside each bowl.

To make the sauce, stir the horseradish mixture into the soy sauce mixture and pour into individual dipping bowls.

Dip the fish into the sauce mixture before eating and eat at once, with the garnish.
Serves 6
Preparation time: 30 minutes

Kamaboko

(Small Fish Cakes)

Kamaboko are very popular in Japan as an hors d'oeuvre, but they can also form part of some one-pot meals as well. A canned version is widely used now, but as always, home-made varieties tend to have a much better taste and texture. Almost any type of firm white fish fillet could be used – or a mixture; this is an excellent way to use leftover fillet pieces. They can also be steamed for a more delicate taste.

Metric/Imperial	American
½kg./1lb. white fish fillets, skinned and chopped	1lb. white fish fillets, skinned and chopped
3 Tbs. flour	3 Tbs. flour
2 egg whites, beaten until frothy	2 egg whites, beaten until frothy
1 Tbs. mirin or sweet sherry	1 Tbs. mirin or sweet sherry
1 tsp. sugar	1 tsp. sugar
½ tsp. monosodium glutamate	½ tsp. MSG
50g./2oz. cornflour	½ cup cornstarch
75ml./3fl.oz. vegetable oil	⅓ cup vegetable oil

Put the fish pieces into a blender and blend until they form a fairly smooth purée. Transfer the purée to a mixing bowl and stir in the flour, egg whites, mirin or sherry, sugar and monosodium glutamate. Beat briskly until the mixture is thoroughly blended.

Take about 2 tablespoonfuls of the mixture and shape it into a small cake or patty shape with your hands. Dust it lightly with the cornflour (cornstarch) and set aside. Repeat the process until all of the mixture is used up.

Heat the oil in a large frying-pan. When it is hot, add the fish cakes (in batches if necessary) and fry gently for 5 minutes on each side, or until they are golden brown and crisp, and cooked through.

Remove from the pan and drain on kitchen towels. Serve hot.

Serves 4-6 as an hors d'oeuvre
Preparation and cooking time: 30 minutes

Shrimps with Bamboo Shoot

Metric/Imperial	American
50ml./2fl.oz. water	¼ cup water
50ml./2fl.oz. soya sauce	¼ cup soy sauce
350g./12oz. shelled prawns	12oz. shelled shrimp
400g./14oz. tin bamboo shoot, drained and sliced	14oz. can bamboo shoot, drained and sliced
2 Tbs. sake or dry sherry	2 Tbs. sake or dry sherry
2 Tbs. mirin or sweet sherry	2 Tbs. mirin or sweet sherry

Put the water and soy sauce into a shallow saucepan and bring to the boil. Reduce the heat to moderate and stir in the prawns (shrimp). Cook for 5 minutes. Using a slotted spoon, transfer the prawns (shrimp) to a warmed bowl and keep hot.

Add the bamboo shoot slices to the pan and return to the boil. Stir in the sake or sherry and mirin or sherry and cook for 3 minutes. Return the prawns (shrimp) to the pan and stir until the mixture is blended. Cook for 1 minute.

Transfer the mixture to a warmed serving dish and serve at once.

Serves 4
Preparation and cooking time: 15 minutes

Iri-Tamago

(Eggs with Shrimp and Peas)

Metric/Imperial	American
4 eggs, lightly beaten	4 eggs, lightly beaten
50ml./2fl.oz. dashi	¼ cup dashi
1 tsp. sugar	1 tsp. sugar
2 tsp. soya sauce	2 tsp. soy sauce
2 tsp. sake or dry sherry	2 tsp. sake or dry sherry
monosodium glutamate (optional)	MSG (optional)
3 Tbs. vegetable oil	3 Tbs. vegetable oil
125g./4oz. frozen shelled shrimps	4 oz. frozen shelled shrimp
225g./8oz. frozen green peas	1 cup frozen green peas
3 dried mushrooms, soaked in cold water for 30 minutes, drained and sliced	3 dried mushrooms, soaked in cold water for 30 minutes, drained and sliced

Beat the eggs, dashi, sugar, soy sauce, sake or sherry and monosodium glutamate to taste together until they are thoroughly blended. Set aside.

Heat the oil in a large frying-pan. When it is hot, add the shrimps, peas and mushrooms and stir-fry for 3 to 4 minutes, or until the shrimps and peas are cooked through. Stir in the eggs and reduce the heat to moderately low. Cook the mixture, stirring the eggs from time to time to 'scramble' them, until the egg mixture has just lightly set.

Transfer the mixture to a warmed serving plate and serve at once.

Serves 2-3
Preparation and cooking time: 40 minutes

Mazezushi

(Vegetables and Seafood with Rice)

Metric/Imperial	American
450g./1lb. short-grain rice	2⅔ cups short-grain rice
600ml./1 pint water	2½ cups water
VINEGAR SAUCE	VINEGAR SAUCE
50ml./2fl.oz. white wine vinegar	¼ cup white wine vinegar
1 Tbs. sugar	1 Tbs. sugar
½ tsp. salt	½ tsp. salt
monosodium glutamate (optional)	MSG (optional)
VEGETABLES	VEGETABLES
2 carrots, thinly sliced	2 carrots, thinly sliced
1 tinned bamboo shoot, drained and thinly sliced	1 canned bamboo shoot, drained and thinly sliced
¼ small turnip, thinly sliced	¼ small turnip, thinly sliced
3 Tbs. frozen green peas	3 Tbs. frozen green peas
175ml./6fl.oz. dashi	¾ cup dashi
1 Tbs. sake or dry sherry	1 Tbs. sake or dry sherry
1 Tbs. sugar	1 Tbs. sugar
1 Tbs. vegetable oil	1 Tbs. vegetable oil
4 dried mushrooms, soaked in cold water for 30 minutes, drained and sliced	4 dried mushrooms, soaked in cold water for 30 minutes, drained and sliced
2 Tbs. soya sauce	2 Tbs. soy sauce
OMELET	OMELET
1 Tbs. vegetable oil	1 Tbs. vegetable oil
3 eggs, lightly beaten	3 eggs, lightly beaten
SEAFOOD	SEAFOOD
125g./4oz. cooked prawns	4oz. cooked shrimp
125g./4oz. crabmeat, shell and cartilage removed and flaked	4oz. crabmeat, shell and cartilage removed and flaked

First make the rice. Cook the rice, following the instructions given in *Gohan*. Transfer the drained rice to a warmed bowl and set aside. To make the vinegar sauce, combine the vinegar, sugar, salt and monosodium glutamate to taste, then pour the mixture over the rice. Stir gently with a wooden spoon and set aside to cool at room temperature.

Meanwhile, prepare the vegetables. Put the carrots, bamboo shoot, turnip and peas into a saucepan and pour over enough water to cover. Bring to the boil and blanch briskly for 2 minutes. Drain the vegetables. Put 125m./4fl. oz. (½ cup) of dashi, the sake or dry sherry and half the sugar in a small saucepan and bring to the boil. Add the drained vegetables and cook for a further 2 minutes. Transfer the vegetables to a bowl and drain and reserve the dashi liquid.

Heat the oil in a small frying-pan. When it is hot, add the mushrooms, the remaining dashi and sugar, and the soy sauce. Cook, stirring constantly, for 3 minutes. Remove from the heat and cool.

To make the omelets, brush the bottom of an omelet pan with some of the oil and pour in about a third of the egg mixture. Tilt the pan so that the mixture covers the bottom of the pan, then leave to cook until the omelet has set. Shake the pan slightly to loosen the omelet, then quickly turn over and cook the other side for 15 seconds. Slide on to a plate and cook the remaining egg mixture in the same way. When all the omelets have been cooked, pile them on top of one another and cut into thin strips.

To assemble, stir the vegetables and reserved cooking liquid gently into the vinegared rice with a wooden spoon. Then stir in the prawns (shrimp) and crabmeat. Arrange the egg strips decoratively over the top and serve at once.
Serves 6
Preparation and cooking time: 2 hours

Hamaguri Shigure-Ni

(Sake and Soy Sauce-Flavoured Clams)

Metric/Imperial	American
50ml./2fl.oz. sake or dry sherry	$\frac{1}{4}$ cup sake or dry sherry
2 Tbs. sugar	2 Tbs. sugar
12 clams, removed from their shells	12 clams, removed from their shells
2 Tbs. soya sauce	2 Tbs. soy sauce

In a large, heavy frying-pan combine the sake or sherry, sugar and clams. Stir the mixture thoroughly with a wooden spoon. Bring to the boil and cook for 3 minutes, stirring constantly. Stir in the soy sauce and boil for a further 1 minute, stirring constantly. Using a slotted spoon, transfer the clams to a plate.

Boil the sauce for a further 10 minutes, or until it becomes thick and rather syrupy. Return the clams to the pan and stir them gently into the sauce. Cook the mixture for about 1 minute, or until the clams are thoroughly coated with the sauce.

Remove from the heat and spoon the mixture into a warmed serving dish. Serve at once.
Serves 4
Preparation and cooking time: 30 minutes

Kimini

(Glazed Prawns or Shrimp)

Metric/Imperial	American
12 medium prawns	12 medium shrimp
50g./2oz. cornflour	$\frac{1}{2}$ cup cornstarch
3$\frac{1}{2}$ Tbs. dashi	3$\frac{1}{2}$ Tbs. dashi
2 Tbs. sake or dry sherry	2 Tbs. sake or dry sherry
$\frac{1}{2}$ tsp. sugar	$\frac{1}{2}$ tsp. sugar
$\frac{1}{4}$ tsp. salt	$\frac{1}{4}$ tsp. salt
monosodium glutamate (optional)	MSG (optional)
3 egg yolks, well beaten	3 egg yolks, well beaten

Shell the prawns (shrimp), leaving the tails intact. Remove the veins at the head with the tip of a knife, then dip the prawns (shrimp) into the cornflour (cornstarch), shaking off any excess. Drop the prawns (shrimp) into a saucepan of boiling water and cook for about 10 seconds. Remove and rinse under cold running water. Set aside.

Pour the dashi into a small saucepan and stir in the sake or sherry, sugar, salt and monosodium glutamate to taste. Bring to the boil. Arrange the prawns (shrimp) in the pan and return the liquid to the boil, basting the prawns (shrimp). When the liquid boils, pour the beaten egg yolks slowly over the prawns (shrimp). Do not stir, cover the pan and simmer over low heat for 2 minutes. Remove from the heat but leave for a further 2 minutes before serving as a side dish, or as a main dish with vegetables.
Serves 2-4
Preparation and cooking time: 20 minutes

Clams are a popular ingredient in many Japanese dishes. In Hamaguri Shigure-Ni they are cooked in a very special mixture of sake and soy sauce.

Kani no Sunomono

(Crab and Cucumber with Vinegar Dressing)

Metric/Imperial	American
½ cucumber	½ cucumber
225g./8oz. crabmeat, shell and cartilage removed and flaked	8oz. crabmeat, shell and cartilage removed and flaked
VINEGAR DRESSING	VINEGAR DRESSING
2 Tbs. white wine vinegar	2 Tbs. white wine vinegar
2 Tbs. mirin or sweet sherry	2 Tbs. mirin or sweet sherry
2 Tbs. dashi	2 Tbs. dashi
1 Tbs. soya sauce	1 Tbs. soy sauce
2 tsp. sugar	2 tsp. sugar
monosodium glutamate (optional)	MSG (optional)

Partially peel the cucumber, leaving some long green strips for colour. Slice as thinly as possible, sprinkle with salt and leave to dégorge in a colander for about 30 minutes. Squeeze out any excess liquid gently with your hands, then dry on kitchen towels. Arrange the cucumber and crabmeat decoratively in a small shallow dish.

To make the vinegar dressing, combine all the ingredients, beating until they are well blended. Pour over the cucumber and crabmeat and toss gently so that they are well coated. Set the dish aside at room temperature to marinate for 30 minutes, tossing gently from time to time. Carefully drain off any excess dressing before serving.

Sunamon ('vinegared things') can accompany main dishes or be served as an hors d'oeuvre.

Serves 2
Preparation time: 1¼ hours

Hamaguri Sakani

(Sake-Flavoured Clams)

Metric/Imperial	American
50ml./2fl.oz. sake or dry sherry	¼ cup sake or dry sherry
12 clams, removed from the shells, half the shells scrubbed and reserved	12 clams, removed from the shells, half the shells scrubbed and reserved
GARNISH	GARNISH
12 lemon slices	12 lemon slices

Put the sake into a large saucepan and bring to the boil. Add the clams, stirring with a wooden spoon. Cover the pan and reduce the heat to low. Simmer for 5 minutes. Using a slotted spoon, remove the clams and arrange one on each of the reserved shells. Garnish each shell with a lemon slice.

Put the clams on a serving dish and allow them to cool to room temperature.

Chill in the refrigerator for 30 minutes. Remove from the refrigerator and serve as an hors d'oeuvre.

Serves 4
Preparation and cooking time: 50 minutes

Torigai to Wakame no Nuta

(Cockles and Seaweed with Miso)

Metric/Imperial	American
1 Tbs. wakame or dried seaweed, soaked in water until soft	1 Tbs. wakame or dried seaweed, soaked in water until soft
8 spring onions, chopped and parboiled	8 scallions, chopped and parboiled

225g./8oz. cockles, washed	8oz. cockles, washed
1 celery stalk, chopped	1 celery stalk, chopped
MISO SAUCE	MISO SAUCE
2½ Tbs. white wine vinegar	2½ Tbs. white wine vinegar
2½ Tbs. sake or dry sherry	2½ Tbs. sake or dry sherry
2½ Tbs. sugar	2½ Tbs. sugar
5 Tbs. miso paste	5 Tbs. miso paste

Put the vinegar, sake and sugar into a saucepan and bring to the boil. Remove from the heat and stir in the miso paste until it melts. Pour into individual dipping bowls and set aside.

Chop the wakame into short lengths, then arrange all the remaining ingredients on one large serving platter or individual serving plates. The sauce can either be served separately or, alternatively, it can be mixed into the ingredients and tossed gently before serving.

This dish is usually served as a starter or a side dish.

Serves 3-4
Preparation and cooking time: 15 minutes

Prawns in Batter

(Korea)

Metric/Imperial	American
½kg./1lb. prawns	1lb. shrimp
vegetable oil for deep-frying	vegetable oil for deep-frying
BATTER	BATTER
50g./2oz. rice flour	½ cup rice flour
salt	salt
monosodium glutamate (optional)	MSG (optional)
1 egg, lightly beaten	1 egg, lightly beaten
125ml./4fl.oz. water	½ cup water
DIPPING SAUCE	DIPPING SAUCE
250ml./8fl.oz. soya sauce	1 cup soy sauce
3 spring onions, chopped	3 scallions, chopped

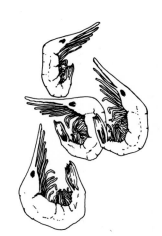

Remove the shells from the prawns (shrimp), leaving the tails intact. Remove the heads and any tentacles.

To make the batter, beat all of the ingredients together in a shallow bowl with a whisk or wooden spoon until they are thoroughly blended.

Set the bowl aside.

Fill a large deep-frying pan one-third full with oil and heat it until it is hot. Dip the prawns (shrimp) first in the batter, coating thoroughly but shaking off any excess, then carefully lower them into the oil, a few at a time. Deep-fry for 2 to 3 minutes, or until the prawns (shrimp) are golden brown. Remove from the oil and drain on kitchen towels. Keep hot while you cook the remaining prawns (shrimp) in the same way.

To make the dipping sauce, combine the soy sauce and spring onions (scallions) and pour into small, individual bowls.

Serve at once, with the prawns (shrimp).

Serves 4
Preparation and cooking time: 25 minutes

ONE-POT

Shin-Sol-Lo

(Korean Steamboat)

This exotic soup-like mixture is the 'royal' dish of Korea and, to be absolutely authentic, should be cooked in a special shin-sol-lo cooker as suggested below. They can be obtained from Chinese or other large Oriental stores. If you don't have one, however, a fondue pot or flameproof casserole makes a perfectly adequate substitute. In the latter case, just put all the ingredients into the pot together and bring to the boil before serving. Any vegetable of your choice can be substituted for those suggested below.

Metric/Imperial	American
FISH	FISH
225g./8oz. firm white fish fillet, skinned and cut into large bite-sized pieces	8oz. firm white fish fillet, skinned and cut into large bite-sized pieces
50g./2oz. cornflour, mixed to a paste with 125ml./4fl.oz. water	½ cup cornstarch, mixed to a paste with ½ cup water
4 Tbs. peanut oil	4 Tbs. peanut oil
VEGETABLES	VEGETABLES
¼ small Chinese cabbage, shredded	¼ small Chinese cabbage, shredded
225g./8oz. leaf spinach, chopped	1⅓ cups chopped leaf spinach
3 carrots, chopped or sliced	3 carrots, chopped or sliced
salt	salt
SHIN-SOL-LO	SHIN-SOL-LO
225g./8oz. cooked meat, such as ox tongue, cut into strips	8oz. cooked meat, such as ox tongue, cut into strips
1 large red pepper, pith and seeds removed and sliced	1 large red pepper, pith and seeds removed and sliced
4 large button mushrooms, sliced	4 large button mushrooms, sliced
2 spring onions, chopped	2 scallions, chopped
125g./4oz. Chinese fish cake, sliced (optional)	4oz. Chinese fish cake, sliced (optional)
125g./4oz. frozen peeled prawns	4oz. frozen peeled shrimp
1.2l./2 pints boiling beef stock	5 cups boiling beef stock
salt and black pepper	salt and black pepper

First prepare the fish. Dip the fish pieces in the cornflour (cornstarch) batter and set aside for 5 minutes. Heat the oil in a large frying-pan. When it is hot, add the fish pieces and fry gently for 5 minutes on each side, or until the flesh just flakes. Remove the fish from the heat and drain on kitchen towels. Transfer the pieces to a plate.

Cook the cabbage, spinach and carrots separately in boiling salted water until they are just cooked but still crisp. Remove from the heat, drain and add to the fish pieces.

To prepare the shin-sol-lo, prepare the charcoal so that it is burning. Arrange the fish pieces, vegetables pieces, then meat, red pepper and mushroom slices around the sides of the pot. Scatter over the spring onions (scallions), fish cake and prawns (shrimp), then pour over the stock and season with salt and pepper to taste.

Put the embers from the charcoal into the centre of the pot, then cover with new charcoal, fanning the embers so that the new charcoal will ignite. Cover the pot and steam the shin-sol-lo for 3 to 5 minutes, or until the stock returns to the boil.

Traditionally, the pot is then brought to the table (with the embers still lit) and diners help themselves. Rice is usually served as an accompaniment, in the same bowl as the shin-sol-lo.

Serves 6–8
Preparation and cooking time: 45 minutes

Sukiyaki I

(Quick-Braised Beef and Vegetables)

Sukiyaki is one of the most popular one-pot dishes in Japan – and is probably the most famous Japanese dish outside the country. To eat it Japanese style, the ingredients for the dish should be arranged decoratively on a serving platter then cooked at the table, fondue-style, with each diner selecting his own food. The cooked food should be dipped in the lightly beaten egg before being eaten.

Metric/Imperial	American
1kg./2lb. fillet steak, cut across the grain into thin slices or strips	2lb. fillet steak, cut across the grain into thin slices or strips
225g./8oz. tin shirataki noodles	8oz. can shirataki noodles
225g./8oz. small spinach leaves	2 cups small spinach leaves
450g./1lb. mushrooms, stalks removed and caps halved	1lb. mushrooms, stalks removed and caps halved
1 large carrot, cut into strips	1 large carrot, cut into strips
12 spring onions, sliced	12 scallions, sliced
200g./7oz. tin bamboo shoot, drained and sliced	7oz. can bamboo shoot, drained and sliced
1 bean curd cake (tofu), cubed	1 bean curd cake (tofu), cubed
250ml./8fl.oz. dashi	1 cup dashi
125ml./4fl.oz. sake or dry sherry	½ cup sake or dry sherry
6 eggs	6 eggs
2 Tbs. beef suet or lard	2 Tbs. beef suet or lard
175ml./6fl.oz. soya sauce	¾ cup soy sauce
2 Tbs. soft brown sugar	2 Tbs. soft brown sugar

Arrange the steak pieces, shirataki noodles, spinach leaves, mushrooms, carrot, spring onions (scallions), bamboo shoot and bean curd cubes decoratively on a large serving platter. Set aside. Mix the dashi and sake together until they are well combined. Set aside. Break the eggs into individual serving bowls and beat lightly. Set aside.

Heat a heavy, flameproof casserole over low heat until it is hot. Spear the suet on a fork and rub gently over the bottom of the casserole, or allow the lard to melt. Discard the suet. Put about a sixth of the meat and vegetables into the casserole, adding about a sixth of the dashi mixture, a sixth of the soy sauce and a sixth of the sugar. Cook for 5 to 6 minutes, stirring and turning frequently, until all the ingredients are tender but still crisp. Using a slotted spoon, transfer the mixture to individual serving plates and serve with the beaten egg. Cook the remaining ingredients in the same way. The liquid should always be simmering. If the food begins to stick in the casserole, add 1 teaspoon of cold water to cool it or to reduce the heat to moderately low. The sauce becomes stronger as more liquid and sugar are added at each cooking stage so it may be necessary to reduce these amounts to your taste.

Serves 6
Preparation and cooking time: 45 minutes

(See over) Sukiyaki is what everyone thinks of when they think of Japanese food, and you can see why when you taste this version (Sukiyaki I). It is also one of the most hospitable of dishes – who can stand on ceremony when faced with a communal pot full of rich, cooking food?

Sukiyaki II

(Marinated Braised Beef and Vegetables)

Metric/Imperial	American
1kg./2lb. fillet steak, cut into thin strips	2lb. fillet steak, cut into thin strips
300ml./10fl.oz. sake or dry sherry	1¼ cups sake or dry sherry
4 Tbs. soya sauce	4 Tbs. soy sauce
salt and pepper	salt and pepper
8 spring onions, cut into 2½cm./1in. lengths	8 scallions, cut into 1in. lengths
12 button mushrooms, stalks removed	12 button mushrooms ,stalks removed
2 large green peppers, pith and seeds removed and cut into strips	2 large green peppers, pith and seeds removed and cut into strips
225g./8oz. small spinach leaves	1 cup small spinach leaves
vegetable oil for deep-frying	vegetable oil for deep-frying
SAUCE	SAUCE
1 eating apple, cored and grated	1 eating apple, cored and grated
1 large leek, cleaned and chopped	1 large leek, cleaned and chopped
2 garlic cloves, crushed	2 garlic cloves, crushed
¼ tsp. cayenne pepper	¼ tsp. cayenne pepper
1 small red pepper, pith and seeds removed and finely chopped	1 small red pepper, pith and seeds removed and finely chopped

Put the beef strips into a large shallow dish and pour over the sake or sherry and soy sauce. Sprinkle over salt and pepper to taste. Set aside at room temperature to marinate for at least 4 hours, turning the meat occasionally. Using a slotted spoon, transfer the meat strips to a plate and reserve the marinade.

Arrange the spring onions (scallions), mushrooms, peppers, and spinach decoratively on a serving platter. Set aside.

Pour the reserved marinade into a serving bowl and stir in the grated apple, leek, garlic, cayenne and red pepper.

Fill a large deep-frying pan one-third full with oil and heat it until it is very hot. Either transfer the oil carefully to a fondue pot or Japanese cooking pot or continue cooking in the saucepan. Carefully lower a few pieces of meat and vegetables into the oil and cook for 1 to 2 minutes, or until they are just crisp. Remove from the oil and drain on kitchen towels. Keep hot while you cook the remaining ingredients in the same way.

The cooked food should be dipped into the sauce before eating.

Serves 6
Preparation and cooking time: 4½ hours

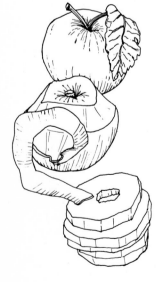

Chiri Nabe

(Fish and Vegetable Casserole)

Metric/Imperial	American
1 small Chinese cabbage, trimmed	1 small Chinese cabbage, trimmed
1 large bream or similar fish, cleaned, gutted and filleted	1 large bream, or similar fish, cleaned, gutted and filleted
3 leeks, cleaned and cut into 1cm./½in. lengths	3 leeks, cleaned and cut into ½in. lengths
3 bean curd cakes (tofu), cubed	3 bean curd cakes (tofu), cubed

1.21/2 pints dashi	5 cups dashi
150ml./5fl.oz. soya sauce	$\frac{2}{3}$ cup soy sauce
6 spring onions, chopped	6 scallions, chopped
1 small turnip, grated	1 small turnip, grated
juice of two lemons	juice of two lemons

Cook the cabbage in boiling water for 5 minutes. Drain, then chop diagonally into 5cm./2in. lengths. Cut the fish into large pieces and arrange the fish, cabbage, leeks and bean curd on a large serving platter.

Pour the dashi into a flameproof casserole or fondue pot and bring to the boil. Add the ingredients to the dashi, a few at a time, and cook for 3 to 5 minutes, or until they are cooked through.

Mix the soy sauce, spring onions (scallions), turnip and lemon juice together and divide among individual dipping bowls. The cooked food should be dipped in the sauce before eating.

Serves 4-6
Preparation and cooking time: 45 minutes

Botan Nabe

(Pork and Vegetables in Stock)

The name for this dish comes from the Japanese word for peony because the pork pieces are arranged in the shape of this flower before cooking.

Metric/Imperial	American
½kg./1lb. carrots, cut into ½cm./¼in. lengths	1lb. carrots, cut into ¼in. lengths
1 medium white cabbage, separated into leaves	1 medium white cabbage, separated into leaves
225g./8oz. mushrooms	2 cups mushrooms
700g./1½lb. lean pork, very thinly sliced	1½lb. lean pork, very thinly sliced
3 garlic cloves, crushed	3 garlic cloves, crushed
4cm./1½in. piece of fresh root ginger, peeled and chopped	1½in. piece of fresh green ginger, peeled and chopped
250ml./8fl.oz. soya sauce	1 cup soy sauce
6 spring onions, finely chopped	6 scallions, finely chopped
2 lemons, cut into small wedges	2 lemons, cut into small wedges
450ml./15fl.oz. dashi	2 cups dashi

Lightly cook the carrots and cabbage separately in boiling water for 3 minutes. Drain and roll up the cabbage leaves into rolls. Arrange the carrots, cabbage rolls and mushrooms decoratively on a serving platter.
Arrange the pork slices carefully in the shape of a flower on a serving plate and garnish with the garlic and ginger to make the centre of the flower.

Combine the soy sauce with about a quarter of the spring onions (scallions) and pour into individual dipping bowls. Arrange the lemon wedges and remaining spring onions (scallions) in separate serving bowls.

Pour the dashi into a saucepan or fondue pot and bring to the boil. Add a few pieces of the pork and cook until it is white. Cook the other ingredients in the same way. The cooked food should be dipped in the sauce before eating.

When all the ingredients have been cooked, the stock may be served as a soup.
Serves 6
Preparation and cooking time: 50 minutes

Tempura

(Deep-Fried Food Japanese Style)

Although tempura is one of the best known Japanese dishes outside Japan, it is not traditionally Japanese – but rather an adaptation of a Portuguese dish. (The name comes from the Latin word for time.) In Japan there are many restaurants devoted exclusively to tempura and in the West it has now become a popular party dish – and it does lend itself extremely well to fondue-style informality.

The oil used to fry the tempura is important; in Japan a mixture of cotton seed, sesame seed and groundnut oil is a favourite and we would suggest here that you use groundnut oil and sesame oil in the proportions of 4 to 1.

Metric/Imperial	American
12 fresh prawns, heads removed but still in shell	12 fresh shrimp, with the heads removed but still in shell
4 plaice fillets, skinned and cut into 2½cm./1in. pieces	4 flounder fillets, skinned and cut into 1in. pieces
1 medium squid, skinned and cut into 2½cm./1in. pieces	1 medium squid, skinned and cut into 1 in. pieces
225g./8oz. cod fillet, skinned and cut into 2½cm./1in. pieces	8oz. cod fillet, skinned and cut into 1in. pieces
1 large green pepper, pith and seeds removed and cut into 2½cm./1in. pieces	1 large green pepper, pith and seeds removed and cut into 1in. pieces
12 small button mushrooms	12 small button mushrooms
1 tinned bamboo shoot, drained and cut into ½cm./¼in. pieces	1 canned bamboo shoot, drained and cut into ¼in. pieces
12 cauliflower flowerets	12 cauliflower flowerets
mixed oil for deep-frying	mixed oil for deep-frying
BATTER	BATTER
1 egg, plus 1 egg yolk, lightly beaten	1 egg, plus 1 egg yolk, lightly beaten
175ml./6fl.oz. water	¾ cup water
125g./4oz. flour	1 cup flour
SAUCE	SAUCE
250ml./8fl.oz. soya sauce	1 cup soy sauce
250ml./8fl.oz. water	1 cup water
2 small turnips or large Japanese radishes, grated	2 small turnips or large Japanese radishes, grated

Put the prawns (shrimp) on a board and slit them lengthways, leaving the tails intact. Remove and discard the shells and open out the flesh so that they stay flat. Arrange the prawns (shrimp), plaice (flounder) pieces, squid, cod, green pepper, mushrooms, bamboo shoot and cauliflower flowerets on a large serving platter.

To make the batter, combine all the batter ingredients and beat with a fork until it forms a smooth paste.

Fill a large deep-frying pan one-third full with the oil and heat it until it is very hot. Either continue cooking in this pan or transfer the oil to a fondue pot and continue cooking over a spirit burner.

Using Japanese cooking chopsticks or a long-handled two-prong fork, spear a piece of food and dip it into the batter. Then carefully lower it into the oil and cook for 2 to 4 minutes, depending on the food being cooked, or until it is golden brown. Remove from the oil and transfer to kitchen towels to drain. Keep hot while you cook the remaining food in the same way.

To make the dipping sauce, combine all the ingredients and pour into individual dipping bowls. The cooked food should be dipped into the sauce before eating.
Serves 8
Preparation and cooking time: 1 hour

Mizataki

(Chicken and Vegetable One-Pot Dish)

Metric/Imperial	American
1 x 1½kg./3lb. chicken, cut through the bones with a cleaver into bite-sized pieces	1 x 3lb. chicken, cut through the bones with a cleaver into bite-sized pieces

1 bean curd cake (tofu), cubed	1 bean curd cake (tofu), cubed
225g./8oz. mushrooms, stalks removed	2 cups mushrooms, stalks removed
1 small cabbage, separated into leaves	1 small cabbage, separated into leaves
4 carrots, thinly sliced	4 carrots, thinly sliced
1 bunch of watercress	1 bunch of watercress
2 leeks, cleaned and cut diagonally into 2½cm./1in. lengths	2 leeks, cleaned and cut diagonally into 1in. lengths
450ml./15fl.oz. dashi	2 cups dashi
250ml./8fl.oz. soya sauce	1 cup soy sauce
lemon slices	lemon slices
grated radish	grated radish

Put the chicken and bean curd on a serving platter. Chop or shred the vegetables attractively and arrange them on a serving platter.

Pour the dashi into a flameproof casserole or fondue pot and bring to the boil. Keep it over low heat and add some chicken and vegetables. Cook for 3 to 5 minutes, or until the meat is just cooked through. Each guest should help himself individually, replenishing the pot as necessary.

Pour the soy sauce into individual dipping bowls and garnish with lemon slices and radish.

The cooked food should be dipped into the sauce before eating.

Serves 4
Preparation and cooking time: 1 hour

Shabu Shabu

(Beef with Cabbage and Spinach)

The name of this dish comes from the sound the ingredients make as they are being cooked in the soup.

Metric/Imperial	American
1 medium white cabbage, separated into leaves	1 medium white cabbage, separated into leaves
12 button mushroom caps	12 button mushroom caps
½kg./1lb. spinach, chopped	3 cups chopped spinach
1 bean curd cake (tofu), cubed	1 bean curd cake (tofu), cubed
700g./1½lb. rump steak, cut across the grain into thin strips	1½lb. rump steak, cut across the grain into thin strips
150ml./5fl.oz. soya sauce	⅔ cup soy sauce
2 radishes, grated	2 radishes, grated
4 spring onions, finely chopped	4 scallions, finely chopped
juice of 2 lemons	juice of 2 lemons
1.2l./2 pints dashi	5 cups dashi

Cook the cabbage leaves lightly for 3 minutes, then drain and remove from the pan. Roll up the leaves into rolls. Arrange all the vegetables and bean curd cubes decoratively on a serving platter. Arrange the beef slices decoratively on a second, smaller platter. Set aside.

Mix the soy sauce, radishes, spring onions (scallions) and lemon juice together and pour into individual dipping bowls.

Pour the dashi into a saucepan or fondue pot and bring to the boil. Cook the ingredients in the stock, a few at a time, until they are just cooked through.

The cooked food should be dipped into the sauce before eating.

Serves 4
Preparation and cooking time: 50 minutes

Yose Nabe

(Chicken and Oyster Casserole)

Yosenabe literally means 'a collection of everything', so the ingredients below are just that – suggestions. Almost anything suitable that takes your fancy could be substituted!

Metric/Imperial	American
900ml./1½ pints dashi	3¾ cups dashi
2 chicken breasts, skinned, boned and cubed	2 chicken breasts, skinned, boned and cubed
2 large carrots, sliced	2 large carrots, sliced
12 radishes, thinly sliced	12 radishes, thinly sliced
50ml./2fl.oz. soya sauce	¼ cup soy sauce
150ml/5fl.oz. sake or dry sherry	⅔ cup sake or dry sherry
225g./8oz. tin shirataki noodles	8oz. can shirataki noodles
3 sheets of nori (seaweed), cubed	3 sheets of nori (seaweed), cubed
8 spring onions, cut into small lengths	8 scallions, cut into small lengths
12 raw prawns, shelled	12 raw shrimp, shelled
18 oysters or clams, shells removed	18 oysters or clams, shells removed
225g./8oz. cod fillet, skinned and cubed	8oz. cod fillet, skinned and cubed
18 button mushroom caps	18 button mushroom caps

Pour the dashi into a large saucepan and bring to the boil. Reduce the heat to low, add the chicken cubes and simmer for 10 minutes, or until the cubes are almost tender. Add the carrots and radishes and simmer for a further 5 minutes. Remove the pan from the heat and transfer the chicken and vegetables to a plate. Strain the stock into a large fondue pot or flameproof casserole and stir in the soy sauce and sake or sherry. Bring to the boil.

Arrange all the remaining ingredients on a large serving platter.

Cook the ingredients in the hot stock for 1 to 2 minutes before eating. When all the ingredients have been cooked, the stock may be served as a soup.

Serves 4
Preparation and cooking time: 1 hour

Oden

(Tokyo Hotchpotch)

Street stalls selling this warming dish – which is supposed to have originated in Tokyo – are a common sight in Japan during winter. It is also an excellent dish for parties since it can be left on very low heat for guests to help themselves as and when they want to eat.

Metric/Imperial	American
2.5l./4 pints dashi	2½ quarts dashi
6 Tbs. soya sauce	6 Tbs. soy sauce
1½ Tbs. sugar	1½ Tbs. sugar
monosodium glutamate (optional)	MSG (optional)
1 large squid, cleaned and cut into rings	1 large squid, cleaned and cut into rings
2 medium turnips, cut into chunks	2 medium turnips, cut into chunks
2 large carrots, cut into chunks	2 large carrots, cut into chunks
4 medium potatoes, cut into chunks	4 medium potatoes, cut into chunks
2 pieces of konnyaku, cut into largish triangles	2 pieces of konnyaku, cut into largish triangles

4 pieces of abura age, cut into largish triangles and parboiled to remove excess oil	4 pieces of abura age, cut into largish triangles and parboiled to remove excess oil
4 hard-boiled eggs	4 hard-cooked eggs
1 bean curd cake (tofu), cubed	1 bean curd cake (tofu), cubed
MEATBALLS	MEATBALLS
350g./12oz. minced beef	12oz. ground beef
2 spring onions, finely chopped	2 scallions, finely chopped
2½cm./1in. piece of fresh root ginger, peeled and grated	1in. piece of fresh green ginger, peeled and grated
1½ Tbs. flour	1½ Tbs. flour
2 tsp. soya sauce	2 tsp. soy sauce
2 small eggs, beaten	2 small eggs, beaten
monosodium glutamate (optional)	MSG (optional)
vegetable oil for deep-frying	vegetable oil for deep-frying

First prepare the meatballs. Combine the beef, spring onions (scallions), ginger, flour, soy sauce, eggs and monosodium glutamate to taste in a large bowl. Using the palm of your hand, gently shape the mixture into small balls, about 2½cm./1in. in diameter.

Fill a large deep-frying pan about one-third full with oil and heat it until it is very hot. Carefully lower the meatballs, a few at a time, into the oil and fry until they are golden brown. Using a slotted spoon, remove the meatballs from the oil and drain on kitchen towels. Keep hot while you fry the remaining meatballs in the same way. Set aside.

Pour the dashi into a large flameproof casserole and add the soy sauce, sugar and monosodium glutamate to taste. Add all the remaining ingredients, including the meatballs but excepting the bean curd, to the pan and bring to the boil. Reduce the heat to very low and simmer for 2 to 3 hours. Add the bean curd about 30 minutes before you wish to serve the dish.

Oden is usually served with mustard to taste.

Serves 8
Preparation and cooking time: 3½ hours

Tempura Harusame

(Deep-Fried Food coated in Harusame Noodle)

Harusame is a Japanese noodle somewhat similar in texture to Chinese cellophane noodles – and these latter can be substituted if harusame is difficult to obtain.

Metric/Imperial	American
8 large prawns, shelled	8 large shrimp, shelled
1 cod fillet, skinned and cut into 5cm./2in. pieces	1 cod fillet, skinned and cut into 2in. pieces
1 large plaice fillet, skinned and cut into 5cm./2in. pieces	1 large flounder fillet, skinned and cut into 2in. pieces
2 scallops, coral removed and quartered	2 scallops, coral removed and quartered
8 button mushrooms	8 button mushrooms
1 tinned bamboo shoot, drained and cut into 5cm./2in. pieces	1 canned bamboo shoot, drained and cut into 2in. pieces
1 carrot, sliced	1 carrot, sliced
50g./2oz. flour	½ cup flour
2 egg whites, well beaten	2 egg whites, well beaten

175g./6oz. harusame, cut into small
   pieces
vegetable oil for deep-frying
SAUCE
175ml./6fl.oz. dashi
2 Tbs. soya sauce
2 Tbs. mirin or sweet sherry
1 tsp. grated daikon or turnip

6oz. harusame, cut into small
   pieces
vegetable oil for deep-frying
SAUCE
¾ cup dashi
2 Tbs. soy sauce
2 Tbs. mirin or sweet sherry
1 tsp. grated daikon or turnip

Arrange the prawns (shrimp), cod, plaice (flounder), scallops, mushrooms, bamboo shoot and carrot on a large platter. Dip them, one by one, first in the flour, shaking off any excess, then in the egg whites and finally roll them in the chopped noodles to coat them thoroughly. Set aside.

Fill a large deep-frying pan about one-third full of vegetable oil and heat it until it is very hot. Carefully lower the food pieces, two or three at a time, into the oil and fry until they are golden brown and the noodles have expanded. Remove from the oil and transfer to kitchen towels to drain. Keep hot while you cook the remaining pieces in the same way.

To make the sauce, put the dashi, soy sauce and mirin or sherry into a saucepan. Bring to the boil, then stir in the grated daikon or turnip. Remove from the heat and pour into a dipping bowl.

Serve the tempura pieces while they are still piping hot, with the dipping sauce.
Serves 6
Preparation and cooking time: 40 minutes

The classic tempura batter contains egg, water and flour but sometimes in Japan there is another ingredient – harusame. Harusame are small white noodles which expand gloriously in the oil when frying and provide the most deliciously crunchy coating for the succulent fish and vegetables being cooked.

VEGETABLES & PICKLES

Tamago Dashimaki

(Rolled Omelet)

Japanese omelet pans (tamago pans) are rectangular in shape, not round as in the West, but a conventional rounded omelet pan can be substituted. If you have a rectangular flameproof griddle, this would be even better.

Metric/Imperial	American
4 eggs, beaten	4 eggs, beaten
125ml./4fl.oz. dashi	½ cup dashi
pinch of salt	pinch of salt
1 tsp. soya sauce	1 tsp. soy sauce
3 Tbs. vegetable oil	3 Tbs. vegetable oil
DIPPING SAUCE	DIPPING SAUCE
50ml./2fl.oz. soya sauce	¼ cup soy sauce
1 tsp. grated daikon, radish or turnip	1 tsp. grated daikon, radish or turnip

First, prepare the dipping sauce. Combine the ingredients together, beating until they are thoroughly blended. Pour into a small dipping bowl and set aside.

Combine the eggs, dashi, salt and soy sauce in a small bowl.

Using a pastry brush, generously brush the surface of an omelet pan with a little of the oil. When the pan is hot, pour in about a third of the egg mixture, tilting the pan so that the mixture runs over the bottom. Reduce the heat to low and cook until the omelet is set. Using tongs or a spatula, carefully roll up the omelet away from you, then slide on to the far side of the pan. Using the pastry brush, grease the vacant part of the pan with some more of the oil and, when it is hot, pour in half the remaining mixture, gently lifting the rolled omelet so that the mixture covers the entire bottom of the pan. Cook again until the omelet is set, then roll up the second omelet as before, enclosing the first omelet within the second one.

Repeat this process, using the remaining oil and remaining egg mixture and again enclosing the rolled-up omelet in a third roll. Carefully slide the completed omelet on to a flat serving dish and cut into thick slices.

Serve at once, with the dipping sauce.

Serves 2–3
Preparation and cooking time: 20 minutes

Cha Soh Juhn

(Vegetable Croquettes)   (Korea)

Metric/Imperial	American
1 large potato, very finely chopped	1 large potato, very finely chopped
2 carrots, coarsely grated	2 carrots, coarsely grated
1 large onion, very finely chopped	1 large onion, very finely chopped
1 garlic clove, crushed	1 garlic clove, crushed
2 eggs, lightly beaten	2 eggs, lightly beaten
50ml./2fl.oz. water	¼ cup water

Metric/Imperial	American
1 Tbs. soya sauce	1 Tbs. soy sauce
½ tsp. salt	½ tsp. salt
75g./3oz. flour	¾ cup flour
50ml./2fl.oz. vegetable oil	¼ cup vegetable oil
SAUCE	SAUCE
50ml./2fl.oz. soya sauce	¼ cup soy sauce
50ml./2fl.oz. wine vinegar	¼ cup wine vinegar
1 Tbs. sugar	1 Tbs. sugar

Put the potato, carrots, onion and garlic into a medium mixing bowl and beat until they are thoroughly blended. In a second bowl, beat the eggs, water, soy sauce and salt together until they are thoroughly blended, then gradually fold in the flour until the mixture forms a smooth batter. Stir in the vegetable mixture until it is well blended.

Heat the oil in a large frying-pan. When it is hot, carefully arrange the mixture in the pan, in heaped tablespoons and fry gently until they are browned on one side. Carefully turn over and fry until the croquettes are golden brown on the other side.

Remove from the oil and drain on kitchen towels.

To make the sauce, combine all the ingredients together in a dipping bowl. Serve the croquettes at once, with the sauce.

Serves 4
Preparation and cooking time: 25 minutes

Ko Chooh Juhn

(Fried Green Peppers)   (Korea)

Metric/Imperial	American
4 green peppers, halved lengthwise and with pith and seeds removed	4 green peppers, halved lengthwise and with pith and seeds removed
225g./8oz. minced beef	8oz. ground beef
1 small onion, very finely chopped	1 small onion, very finely chopped
1 garlic clove, crushed	1 garlic clove, crushed
1 Tbs. soya sauce	1 Tbs. soy sauce
¼ tsp. hot chilli powder	¼ tsp. hot chilli powder
1 tsp. roasted sesame seeds, ground	1 tsp. roasted sesame seeds, ground
2 eggs, lightly beaten	2 eggs, lightly beaten
25g./1oz. flour	¼ cup flour
50ml./2fl.oz. vegetable oil	¼ cup vegetable oil
DIPPING SAUCE	DIPPING SAUCE
125ml./4fl.oz. soya sauce	½ cup soy sauce
125ml./4fl.oz. wine vinegar	½ cup wine vinegar
1 garlic clove, crushed	1 garlic clove, crushed

Put the pepper halves into a large saucepan and just cover with water. Bring to the boil and blanch the peppers for 5 minutes. Drain and set them aside while you make the filling.

Put the beef, onion, garlic, soy sauce, chilli powder and sesame seeds into a mixing bowl and beat them until they are thoroughly blended. Spoon the beef mixture into the pepper halves until they are level with the edges. Carefully dip the pepper halves in the beaten eggs, then in the flour, shaking off any excess. Set aside.

To make the dipping sauce, combine all the ingredients in a small bowl,

beating until they are thoroughly blended. Pour into a dipping bowl.

Heat the oil in a large frying-pan. Fry gently for 10 to 15 minutes, turning the peppers occasionally, or until the meat is cooked through.

Remove from the pan and serve at once, accompanied by the dipping sauce.

Serves 4
Preparation and cooking time: 30 minutes

Kong-Na-Mool

(Bean Sprouts)   (Korea)

Metric/Imperial	American
1kg./2lb. bean sprouts	4 cups bean sprouts
2 tsp. soya sauce	2 tsp. soy sauce
1 Tbs. roasted sesame seeds, ground	1 Tbs. roasted sesame seeds, ground
salt	salt
2 spring onions, green part only, finely chopped	2 scallions, green part only, finely chopped
1 tsp. sesame oil	1 tsp. sesame oil

Put the bean sprouts into a saucepan and cover with boiling water. Cook for 5 to 10 minutes, or until they are just tender. Drain and return the bean sprouts to the pan.

Stir in the remaining ingredients, a little at a time, and cook over moderate heat until all are combined.

Serve at once.

Serves 6
Preparation and cooking time: 15 minutes

Umani

(Vegetables Simmered in Soy Sauce)

Metric/Imperial	American
2 carrots, sliced diagonally into short lengths	2 carrots, sliced diagonally into short lengths
200g./7oz. tin bamboo shoot, drained and cut into 5cm./2in. lengths	7oz. can bamboo shoot, drained and cut into 2in. lengths
200g./7oz. tin konnyaku, cut into 5cm./2in. cubes	7 oz. can konnyaku, cut into 2in. cubes
600ml./1 pint dashi	2½ cups dashi
5 Tbs. soya sauce	5 Tbs. soy sauce
2 Tbs. sugar	2 Tbs. sugar
1 Tbs. mirin or sweet sherry	1 Tbs. mirin or sweet sherry
1 tsp. salt	1 tsp. salt
6 dried mushrooms, soaked in cold water for 30 minutes, drained, and stalks removed	6 dried mushrooms, soaked in cold water for 30 minutes, drained and stalks removed

125g./4oz. French beans, chopped	⅔ cup chopped green beans
MEATBALLS	MEATBALLS
½kg./1lb. minced beef	1lb. ground beef
1 Tbs. soya sauce	1 Tbs. soy sauce
1 Tbs. mirin or sweet sherry	1 Tbs. mirin or sweet sherry
2 Tbs. cornflour	2 Tbs. cornstarch
3 Tbs. dashi	3 Tbs. dashi

First make the meatballs. Combine all the ingredients in a large mixing bowl. Using the palm of your hands, gently shape the mixture into balls about 5cm./2in. in diameter. Set aside.

Put the carrots, bamboo shoot and konnyaku into a saucepan and add the dashi, soy sauce, sugar, mirin or sherry and salt. Bring to the boil, then reduce the heat to low. Add the meatballs to the pan, cover and simmer for 15 minutes. Add the mushroom caps and French (green) beans to the pan and simmer for a further 10 minutes.

Serve as a vegetable side dish, hot or cold.
Serves 4-6
Preparation and cooking time: 1¼ hours

Yasi no Kushiage

(Vegetable Shis-kebab)

Metric/Imperial	American
3 eggs, lightly beaten	3 eggs, lightly beaten
50g./2oz. dry breadcrumbs	⅔ cup dry breadcrumbs
flour for coating	flour for coating
½ medium cauliflower, separated into small flowerets	½ medium cauliflower, separated into small flowerets
125g./4oz. mushroom caps	1 cup button mushroom caps
2 courgettes, sliced	2 zucchini, sliced
2 onions, cut downwards into 8 pieces	2 onions, cut downwards into 8 pieces
vegetable oil for deep-frying	vegetable oil for deep-frying
SAUCE	SAUCE
1 Tbs. miso paste	1 Tbs. miso paste
1 tsp. vinegar	1 tsp. vinegar
150ml./5fl.oz. mayonnaise	⅔ cup mayonnaise

First make the sauce. Beat the miso paste and vinegar together until they are well blended, then stir into the mayonnaise. Set aside while you cook the vegetables.

Put the eggs, breadcrumbs and flour into separate, shallow bowls. Dip all of the vegetable pieces first in the eggs, then in the flour and finally in the breadcrumbs, shaking off any excess.

Arrange the pieces on to metal skewers, repeating on different skewers until they are used up. (The skewers will be put into a large saucepan, so make sure the vegetables are arranged in such a way that they can be deep-fried.)

Fill a large deep-frying pan about one-third full with oil and heat it until it is very hot. Carefully lower the skewers into the hot oil and fry until the vegetables are deep golden. Remove the skewers from the oil and drain on kitchen towels.

Arrange the vegetable kebabs on serving platters and either pour over the sauce or serve it as an accompaniment. Serve at once.
Serves 4
Preparation and cooking time: 45 minutes

(See over) Pride of place in this picture is given to Yasi no Kushiage (Vegetable Shis-kebab)– delightfully filling and savoury kebabs which can be a light meal on their own, or be served perhaps with some Sashimi or other light fish dish. Also in the picture are Carrot Salad and Goma Joyu Ae (Green Beans with Sesame Dressing).

Niyakko Tofu

(Cold Bean Curd)

Metric/Imperial	American
4 bean curd cakes (tofu)	4 bean curd cakes (tofu)
GARNISH	GARNISH
2 garlic cloves, crushed	2 garlic cloves, crushed
2½cm./1in. piece of fresh root ginger, peeled and grated	1in. piece of fresh green ginger, peeled and grated
4 mint leaves, chopped	4 mint leaves, chopped
½ leek, cleaned and sliced into thin strips	½ leek, cleaned and sliced into thin strips
DIPPING SAUCE	DIPPING SAUCE
75ml./3fl.oz. soya sauce	6 Tbs. soy sauce
1½ Tbs. sake or dry sherry	1½ Tbs. sake or dry sherry
monosodium glutamate (optional)	MSG (optional)

Cut the bean curd into small cubes and divide among individual serving bowls. Add chilled water, so that the bean curd cubes are floating.

Arrange the garlic, ginger, mint and leek decoratively on a small serving dish. Combine all the ingredients for the sauce in a small mixing bowl, then divide among individual small dipping bowls.

To serve, each diner sprinkles the garnish offerings to taste into the dipping sauce, and dips in the bean curd cubes before eating.

Serves 4
Preparation time: 10 minutes

Shirasu Ae

(Vegetables Mixed in White Sesame Sauce)

This dish originated with Zen monks in Japan and is considered an exercise in skill to prepare – but although it is a little time-consuming, the end result is well worth the effort. The 'secret' of making good Shirasu Ae is to remove as much water from the vegetables as possible.

Metric/Imperial	American
175g./6oz. dried broad white beans, soaked overnight	1 cup dried lima beans, soaked overnight
2 medium aubergines	2 medium eggplants
5 Tbs. water	5 Tbs. water
2 Tbs. soya sauce	2 Tbs. soy sauce
2 tsp. sugar	2 tsp. sugar
4 dried mushrooms, soaked in cold water for 30 minutes, drained, stalks removed and caps thinly sliced	4 dried mushrooms, soaked in cold water for 30 minutes, drained, stalks removed and caps thinly sliced
SESAME SAUCE	SESAME SAUCE
½ bean curd cake (tofu), boiled for 3 minutes and drained	½ bean curd cake (tofu), boiled for 3 minutes and drained
4 Tbs. white sesame seeds	4 Tbs. white sesame seeds
1 Tbs. sugar	1 Tbs. sugar

3 Tbs. vinegar	3 Tbs. vinegar
1 Tbs. mirin or sweet sherry	1 Tbs. mirin or sweet sherry
½ tsp. salt	½ tsp. salt

First prepare the dressing. Put the drained bean curd into a cloth and gently squeeze out as much water as possible (the bean curd should break up). Set aside. Gently fry the sesame seeds in a small frying-pan until they begin to 'jump', taking care not to burn them too much. Remove from the heat and put them into a mortar. Grind with a pestle until the seeds form a paste (this may take some time – so be prepared!). Stir the bean curd into the mortar and continue to pound with the pestle for a further 3 minutes. Stir in the remaining sauce ingredients and continue pounding until the sauce is smooth and sticky and makes a sort of suction noise when the pestle is moved around the mortar. Set aside.

Meanwhile, prepare the vegetables. Put the beans and their soaking liquid into a small saucepan and bring to the boil. Reduce the heat to moderately low and cook for about 1 hour, or until they are tender. Replenish the liquid if necessary during cooking. Cook the aubergines (eggplants) in boiling salted water for 1 hour or until they are tender. Drain and transfer to a chopping board. Cut the aubergines (eggplants) lengthways into thin slices, then halve each round to make a half-moon shape. Set aside.

Put the water, soy sauce and sugar into a small saucepan and bring to the boil, stirring constantly until the sugar dissolves. Add the mushroom slices to the pan, reduce the heat to low and simmer for 10 minutes, so that the mushrooms absorb the flavour of the liquid. Drain the mushrooms and put into a cloth. Gently squeeze as much liquid as possible out of the mushrooms.

To serve, combine all the vegetables together, then pour over the sesame sauce. Stir gently to coat the vegetables in the sauce and serve the dish at room temperature.

Serves 6

Preparation and cooking time: 1½ hours

Carrot Salad

Metric/Imperial	American
4 carrots, scraped	4 carrots, scraped
2 Japanese radishes (daikon), peeled	2 Japanese radishes (daikon), peeled
1 tsp. salt	1 tsp. salt
150ml./5fl.oz. cider vinegar	10 Tbs. cider vinegar
2 Tbs. sugar	2 Tbs. sugar
1 Tbs. soya sauce	1 Tbs. soy sauce
1cm./½in. piece of fresh root ginger, peeled and chopped	½in. piece of fresh green ginger, peeled and chopped
monosodium glutamate (optional)	MSG (optional)

Carefully cut the carrots and radishes into long, thin strips. Arrange in a bowl, sprinkle with the salt and set aside for 45 minutes. Drain off any water which appears on the surface of the vegetables and dry on kitchen towels. Transfer the vegetable strips to a shallow serving bowl.

Put all the remaining ingredients into a screw-top jar and shake vigorously to mix. Pour the dressing over the salad and serve at once.

Serves 4

Preparation time: 1 hour

Note: Turnip can be substituted for the daikon if they are not available.

Goma Joyu Ae

(French [Green] Beans with Sesame Dressing)

Metric/Imperial	American
350g./12oz. French beans, chopped	2 cups chopped green beans
DRESSING	DRESSING
4 Tbs. sesame seeds	4 Tbs. sesame seeds
2 Tbs. soya sauce	2 Tbs. soy sauce
1 Tbs. sugar	1 Tbs. sugar
monosodium glutamate (optional)	MSG (optional)

Cook the beans in lightly salted boiling water for about 5 minutes, or until they are just tender. Drain, then rinse in cold water. Dry on kitchen towels and set aside.

Roast the sesame seeds gently in a small pan until they begin to 'jump' then pound in a mortar with a pestle to release the oil – this takes some time. When they form a reasonably smooth paste, stir in the soy sauce, sugar and monosodium glutamate to taste.

Arrange the beans in a serving dish and spoon over the dressing. Mix gently, making sure the beans are well coated. Serve at once, as a side dish.
Serves 4
Preparation and cooking time: 20 minutes

Mixed Vegetable Salad

(Korea)

Metric/Imperial	American
1 small turnip	1 small turnip
1 tsp. salt	1 tsp. salt
3 Tbs. sesame oil	3 Tbs. sesame oil
1 small onion, finely chopped	1 small onion, finely chopped
125g./4oz. mushrooms, sliced	1 cup sliced mushrooms
2 celery stalks, thinly sliced	2 celery stalks, thinly sliced
3 spring onions, thinly sliced	3 scallions, thinly sliced
1 carrot, cut into thin strips	1 carrot, cut into thin strips
DRESSING	DRESSING
3 Tbs. soya sauce	3 Tbs. soy sauce
1 Tbs. soft brown sugar	1 Tbs. soft brown sugar
1 Tbs. vinegar	1 Tbs. vinegar
½ tsp. ground ginger	½ tsp. ground ginger
1 Tbs. finely chopped pine nuts	1 Tbs. finely chopped pine nuts

Cut the turnip into long, thin strips, then sprinkle over the salt. Set aside for 15 minutes.

Heat the oil in a small frying-pan. When it is hot, add the turnip strips and fry for 3 to 4 minutes, turning occasionally, or until they are crisp. Transfer to kitchen towels to drain. Add the onion to the pan and fry until it is golden brown. Transfer to kitchen towels to drain. Add the mushrooms and fry them for 4 minutes, stirring frequently. Transfer to kitchen towels to drain. Finally, fry the celery in the pan for 3 minutes, then transfer to kitchen towels. Put all the vegetables in a bowl and leave until they are cold.

Stir in the spring onions (scallions) and carrot. Combine all the dressing

ingredients, then pour over the mixture. Toss lightly before serving.
Serves 4
Preparation and cooking time: 2 hours

Horeso no Chitashi

(Boiled Spinach)

Metric/Imperial	American
½kg./1lb. spinach leaves, washed	1lb. spinach leaves, washed
1 Tbs. katsuobushi or dried tuna	1 Tbs. katsuobushi or dried tuna
1 Tbs. soya sauce	1 Tbs. soy sauce
Monosodium glutamate (optional)	MSG (optional)

Put the spinach into a saucepan. Do *not* add water (the water clinging to the leaves will be sufficient). Cook gently for 6 to 8 minutes, or until the spinach is tender, taking care not to overcook. Drain, then arrange the spinach on a chopping board so that all the stalks are facing the same way. Shred the spinach, crosswise, into 2½cm./1in. sections. Section by section, gently squeeze out the water from the spinach.

Arrange the dry spinach on a serving plate and sprinkle over the katsuobushi, soy sauce and monosodium glutamate to taste. Serve cold, as a side dish with meat or fish.
Serves 4
Preparation and cooking time: 20 minutes
Note: Watercress or cos (romaine) lettuce can be cooked in this way.

A delicious, filling dish from Korea is Mixed Vegetable Salad. This version contains turnip, carrot, celery, mushrooms and spring onions (scallions), but you can add your favourite vegetables as you wish.

Kabu no Tsukemono

(Pickled Turnip)

Metric/Imperial	American
1 large turnip, sliced as thinly as possible	1 large turnip, sliced as thinly as possible
1 piece of kombu (seaweed), about 2½ x 5cm./1 x 2in.	1 piece of kombu (seaweed), about 1 x 2in.
4cm./1½in. piece of fresh root ginger, peeled and sliced	1½in. piece of fresh green ginger, peeled and sliced
2 dry red chillis, chopped	2 dry red chillis, chopped
chopped rind of ½ lemon	chopped rind of ½ lemon
½ carrot, cut into matchstick strips	½ carrot, cut into matchstick strips
2 tsp. salt	2 tsp. salt
DRESSING	DRESSING
1 Tbs. mirin or sweet sherry	1 Tbs. mirin or sweet sherry
1 Tbs. soya sauce	1 Tbs. soy sauce

Put the turnip, kombu, ginger, red chillis, lemon rind, carrot and salt into a deep plate. Cover and place a heavy object, such as an iron on top to compress the mixture. Leave for at least 12 hours.

To serve, remove the heavy object and uncover. Using your hands, gently squeeze any excess moisture from the pickle. Transfer to a serving bowl and pour over the soy sauce and mirin or sherry. Toss gently to mix and serve at once.
Serves 4
Preparation time: 12¼ hours

Kim Chee I

(Pickled Cabbage)

Metric/Imperial	American
1 large celery or Chinese cabbage, shredded	1 large celery or Chinese cabbage, shredded
125g./4oz. rock salt	½ cup rock salt
900ml./1½ pints water	3¾ cups water
6 spring onions, finely chopped	6 scallions, finely chopped
2 tsp. sugar	2 tsp. sugar
5cm./2in. piece of fresh root ginger, peeled and cut into strips	2in. piece of fresh green ginger peeled and cut into strips
2 chillis, finely chopped	2 chillis, finely chopped

Put the shredded cabbage in a large bowl and sprinkle over the salt. Pour over the water, cover and set aside overnight.

Combine the spring onions (scallions), sugar, ginger and chillis.

Drain, then rinse and drain the cabbage again. Put the cabbage in a fresh bowl and stir in the spring onion (scallion) mixture. Pack into sterilized pickling jars, cover and set aside for 4 to 5 days before using.
Makes about 1.2l./2 pints (5 cups)
Preparation time: 6 days

Kim Chee II

(Pickled Cabbage)   (Korea)

Metric/Imperial	American
1 Chinese cabbage, quartered	1 Chinese cabbage, quartered
3 Tbs. salt	3 Tbs. salt
2 tsp. hot chilli powder	2 tsp. hot chilli powder
2 garlic cloves, crushed	2 garlic cloves, crushed
4 spring onions, chopped	4 scallions, chopped
1 small onion, chopped	1 small onion, chopped
1 small carrot, chopped	1 small carrot, chopped
1 Tbs. sugar	1 Tbs. sugar
1 large ripe pear, peeled, cored and roughly chopped	1 large ripe pear, peeled, cored and roughly chopped
monosodium glutamate (optional)	MSG (optional)

Put the cabbage into a large shallow bowl and sprinkle over the salt. Leave overnight to dégorge.

Remove the cabbage from the bowl and wash under cold running water. Squeeze all the moisture from the cabbage with your hands, then shred finely.

Put the cabbage, and all the remaining ingredients, into a large jar or deep bowl and cover with a heavy weight. Set aside for 1 to 2 days before serving.

Serves 8
Preparation time: 3 days

Na-Moul

(Spinach Pickle)   (Korea)

Metric/Imperial	American
1kg./2lb. leaf spinach	2lb. leaf spinach
2 garlic cloves, crushed	2 garlic cloves, crushed
1 Tbs. roasted sesame seeds, ground	1 Tbs. roasted sesame seeds, ground
1 Tbs. sesame oil	1 Tbs. sesame oil
2 spring onions, finely chopped	2 scallions, finely chopped
1 tsp. hot chilli powder	1 tsp. hot chilli powder

Wash the spinach thoroughly in cold, running water. Put into a saucepan and bring to the boil (do not add any more water – the water clinging to the leaves will make enough liquid). Reduce the heat to low and cook the spinach for 5 to 8 minutes, or until it is tender. Remove the saucepan from the heat and drain the spinach very thoroughly, squeezing as much moisture from the leaves as possible.

Transfer the drained spinach to a shallow serving dish. Stir in all of the remaining ingredients until the mixture is well blended. Set aside at room temperature for 3 hours before serving.

Serves 8
Preparation and cooking time: 3¼ hours

GLOSSARY

Abure age Fried bean curd, usually sold in thin, frozen sheets. Obtainable from Japanese stores. Substitute other types of bean curd, as available – but the taste will be different.

Agar-agar A gelatinous substance obtained from seaweed, widely used in Japanese cooking. Used as a substitute setting gel in vegetarian cooking. Obtainable from oriental and health food stores. If unavailable (and you are not a vegetarian) substitute gelatine (gelatin).

Aji-no-moto The Japanese word for monosodium glutamate (MSG), which is widely used as a catalyst substance in cooking. For ease of reference, it is always referred to by its English name in this book. Obtainable from oriental stores and most supermarkets. It can safely be omitted from recipes if you prefer.

Bean curd Bean curd, called tofu in Japan, is made from soya beans and is an important ingredient in most oriental cuisines. Sold fresh, in shimmering, white 'cakes'. Store fresh bean curd in water in the refrigerator; keeps for two to three days. Also available canned. When canned bean curd is opened, treat as for fresh. For ease of reference, both English and Japanese names are given in this book. Obtainable from Chinese, Japanese and all other oriental stores.

Daikon A mild, long white radish very popular throughout Japan. Used both in cooking and as a garnish, and somewhat resembles the parsnip in appearance, although it is much paler in colour. Sometimes available from Chinese or Japanese stores. If unobtainable, small white turnips may be substituted.

Dashi The basic stock of all Japanese cooking (see recipe). It is now often made from an instant powder in Japan called dashi-no-moto. The powder can be obtained in Japanese super-markets. If unavailable, chicken stock can be substituted.

Ginger Ginger is used extensively throughout the orient, and usually in its knobbly, root form rather than ground. To use fresh (green) ginger root, remove the brown skin and woody areas and chop the moist flesh. To store, either wrap tightly, unpeeled, in plastic film, or cover with dry sherry. Always keep in the refrigerator. Stored in this way it will keep for about six weeks. *In extremis* ground ginger can be substituted (although the taste is quite definitely not the same) – about ½ teaspoon equals a 4cm./1½in. piece of fresh (green) ginger root. Ginger is available from all oriental stores and some specialty vegetable shops.

Ginko nuts (Also called ginnan in Japan) the kernels of the maidenhair tree. Used both as a flavouring and an ingredient in Japanese cooking. Available canned from Japanese stores. If it is unobtainable, omit from the recipe.

Ginseng Many drinks are made from the root of the ginseng plant. In Korea, the tea made from ginseng is very popular and many miraculous – and aphrodisiac – properties are attributed to it. Several liquors of varying strength are also made from the plant.

Hichimi togarashi A seven-flavour spice used as a garnish in Japanese cooking. It is darkish red in colour. Available from Japanese stores. If unobtainable, substitute paprika.

Kanpyo Dried gourd strips used as an ingredient in Japanese cooking. Available only from Japanese stores. No substitute.

Katsuobushi Katsuobushi are dried bonito (tuna fish) flakes, one of the basic ingredients in a proper dashi stock. Sold in flake form from Japanese general stores. There is no substitute.

Kombu A dried kelp, a sort of seaweed, sold in greyish-black ribbon blocks. Used as a flavouring in dashi and also to flavour vinegared rice (sushi). Available from Japanese or other oriental stores and health food shops.

Konnyaku Small, gelatinous white cakes, sold canned in Japanese or oriental stores. Often added to soups, chopped into bite-sized pieces. There is no substitute.

Mirin A sweet Japanese rice wine used only for cooking. If unobtainable sweet or medium sherry can be substituted. Available from Japanese stores.

Miso Miso is a fermented, dark grey paste made from cooked soya beans. Often added to dashi to make a thicker, more substantial stock for soups and dips. Miso is sold in plastic packs from Japanese stores or health food shops.

Noodles	Noodles of one type or another are very popular in Japanese cooking. There are four main types: *harusame* the equivalent of Chinese cellophane noodles, which are usually either soaked and added to recipes or deep-fried; *soba*, thin, green-brown noodles made from buckwheat flour; *somen*, fine white noodles, used in the same way as vermicelli – if they are unavailable, vermicelli can be used as a substitute; and *udon*, thicker noodles made from white flour – spaghetti makes an acceptable equivalent if they are unavailable.
Nori	Dried laver, an edible form of seaweed, is one of the most popular garnishes in Japanese cooking. Usually toasted until crisp, then crumbled over ingredients such as rice or noodles. It is available in blackish sheets from Japanese stores and some health food shops.
Sake	Japan's favourite rice wine, a dryish, greyish liquid that seems milder than it is. Used extensively in cooking, particularly in marinades and dipping sauces. Substitute dry sherry or dry white wine if unobtainable. Available usually from Japanese and other oriental stores and also better liquor stores.
Sesame seed	Used extensively as a flavouring in both Japanese and Korean cooking. In Japan it is usually toasted then pounded in a mortar until it releases its oil; in Korea it is roasted then ground and sprinkled over practically everything.
Shiitake	The Japanese form of dried mushrooms, a delicacy popular throughout the Orient. Available from Japanese or other oriental stores. If unavailable substitute Chinese dried mushrooms – and always treat in the same way, that is, soak in cold water for 30 minutes, drain and remove stalks before using. Do not substitute European dried mushrooms – the taste is completely different.
Shirataki	A type of transparent noodle made not from flour but from the starch of vegetable plants. Usually sold canned in Japanese stores. No substitute.
Soy sauce	Yet another product of the ubiquitous soya bean plant, and used by almost every cuisine in the Orient. In Japan, a lighter slightly less salty soy sauce (called shoyu) is used and if you are cooking Japanese food this version should be used if possible. Koreans use both the Chinese and Japanese versions, according to the dish being cooked.
Wakame	A type of dried seaweed. It is sold, dried, in ribbon strands in Japanese stores and some health food shops.
Wasabe	A green horseradish powder very popular as a garnish and as an ingredient in dipping sauces in Japan. Usually sold in tins and served mixed to a paste with cold water – see specific recipes for proportions. Sold in Japanese stores and some better supermarkets. If unavailable, substitute western horseradish or mustard paste.

RECIPE INDEX